The
X
Press

Presents

KARLINE SMITH'S

Moss Side
MASSIVE

Published by
THE X PRESS, 55 BROADWAY MARKET, LONDON E8 4PH.
TEL: 081 985 0797

Distributed by Turnaround, 27 Horsell Road, London N5 1XL
Tel: 071 609 7836

Printed by BPC Paperbacks Ltd, Aylesbury, Bucks.

This book is for my children, Isaac and Tamaiya Hodges, and my sister's children, Sharma and Joshua Walfall.

Acknowledgments:

Mum and Dad, respect due to the max.

*Special mention to
JENNIFER, LORRAINE and TRACY. JAH RAS
TAFARI.
Special thanks to DAWN FERARRIO, my ex-English
teacher at school, who wholeheartedly encouraged me.
BRENDA keep singing. MARCUS NAPHTALI. Thanks
to FRONTLINE RADIO, UNITYFRESH, STING
RADIO, SOUL NATION, LOVE ENERGY and all
other Manchester pirate radio stations.*

*Thanks to all my friends, Janet Benjamin of
Manchester and Janet Johnson, Sandra Smith, Joanne
Swaby, Pat Daye (for telling me to write a novel), Jackie
Barnett, Merle Levi. All my homegirls Carol Atta,
Fiona, Sadie Malcolm, Versil Pemberton. To homeboys
and brethren, OSSIE P, Milky, Paul Levi, Cabb-I
YOUT, Ron-I, Mister C. Special mention to IAN LEVI.*

THE PIPER MILL POSSE

Fluxy
Bluebwai
Teeko
Marvin 'Jigsy' Ellis
Easy
Slim

THE GRANGE CREW

Storm
Lewty
Colours
Frenchie
Snapper
Lick-Shot
Sly
Rough-Cut

T HE CAR EASED to a stop on Bonsall Street in Hulme. The driver, a tall, slim, dark-skinned youth, with a broad forehead below a gleaming mop of short and neat processed hair, narrow sideburns and a whisper of a beard, glanced in the rearview mirror as he turned the engine off. A confident smile revealed a gold-capped tooth and a single dimple on his left cheek. With one hand, he undid the top button of his collarless black shirt and flicked a speck of dust off the lapel of his smart, pastel-coloured suit.

"You sure you don't want me to cover you?" the fair-skinned younger boy in the passenger seat asked, his face serious.

Fluxy smiled. "Just settle," he reassured, "I'm only going to the shop."

Fluxy had to give the boy his props. Bluebwai had proved to be a reliable soldier. At seventeen he was just a 'yout', but he was sharp and loyal to the bone.

He opened the door of his sleek, new model Mercedes, leaving the keys in the ignition and the radio still tuned to Frontline, the local pirate. He shivered as he stepped out into the early afternoon autumn chill and remembered that Blue, like most youths his age, loved the gangsta rap business. Gangsta rap was alright but Fluxy preferred to have a little more flavour in his ear. Like Buju or Top Cat or a sound tape from Yard.

"Just watch my car," he told Blue, "I don't want no pickney distressing it, seen?"

Fluxy pushed the driver's door shut behind him and made his way forward, smiling furtively and pulling a stylish pair of sunglasses out of his breast pocket, despite the cold. He had good reason to skin teeth. He was doing exceptionally well and at 21 years of age he nearly had it all: two powerful cars, women, an apartment full of lavish furniture and designer clothes. It was that sort of thing that gave him respect in his neighbourhood. The reason he got involved with the drugs in the first place was because of the money. And he wasn't kidding himself, he knew it wasn't a career, that you can't spend your whole life selling drugs, because it doesn't lead anywhere. But for the moment he was high rollin', and that was a fact! He was livin' large and the younger youths like Blue looked up to him. They wanted to be like him because there was nothing else to be, not in their neighbourhood anyway.

Fluxy would almost burst out laughing when he thought about his school days. Yeah, if those teachers could see him now they would choke. They couldn't wait to see the back of him when he got expelled, but he'd made it. Now he was earning more money in a month than they earned in a year.

After school he had chosen what he knew best, the

2

streets. They were the university of life, an education you couldn't pay for. He had no regrets. With the money he was making, he could afford to indulge his taste for flash dressing in silk shirts and the very latest two-pieces out of New York. But this wasn't New York. It was Moss Side, Manchester. The Moss is where it's going down, he thought. He laughed aloud. It was a dirty game he was in, but that didn't bother him. The way he saw it Piper Mill crew were a security firm. It always amused him when he told people that he made a living 'providing security', but at the end of the day that's what they did. And they had to charge for their services. Those businesses which were unwilling to be taxed had themselves to blame if robbers tested them. They also provided security for the safe distribution of drugs in their area. In truth, they controlled the runnings. Right now, drugs money was talking so loud that, in his head, Fluxy had made a mental calculation of potential profits should Piper Mill expand throughout the city.

Fluxy was content with his life. Almost. Things had been going so well lately, but that didn't stop him from wanting more. The only way to get more was to branch further afield, to control more territories. But there was one little problem.

Storm, the leader of his rival gang, the Grange. The single most dangerous threat to his livelihood. Of all the enemies Fluxy had made a habit of collecting in his short, dizzying life, Storm was the most frustrating. The Grange Close crew controlled most of the territories on the Alexandra Park Estate, one of the biggest housing estates in Europe, Fluxy had learned at school. They also wanted to expand and had encroached on Piper Mill territory on more than one occasion. More pressing was the fact that Storm had demanded a percentage of Piper Mill takings. It was an insult Fluxy was not prepared to forget. His crew would have no respect for him if he allowed Storm to go unpunished. An insult like this always spread like wildfire through the estates. Everybody was awaiting Piper Mill's response. But Piper Mill weren't ready to take on the Grange and Fluxy knew it. His younger brother, Jigsy, was so incensed by the insult that he was less concerned about the Grange being a larger posse in numbers, or that they always seemed to have the best when it came to firearms. As far as Jigsy was concerned, no 'bwai' was going to test Piper Mill and get away with it.

For a moment, the thought crossed Fluxy's mind that this thing was too big for even him to control. Things were already tense on the streets between the gangs. Recently, whenever a Piper Mill man bucked up on a Grange man in any situation things got seriously heated. Already an altercation at a blues dance had resulted in one Piper Mill and one Grange member in intensive care. They both only just made it to the hospital — their stomachs punctured with knife wounds. Fluxy knew he would have to get rid of Storm somehow, before the Grange destroyed everything he'd built up. That was the nature of this business. Tough gangsta shit meant dog eat dog. Fluxy frowned. He didn't fancy himself as dog food.

Maybe it was the thought of Storm that bothered him but, despite the calm, he began to feel uneasy, as if something wasn't quite right. He turned his head

4

around briefly and saw his Mercedes gleaming behind him. He could still hear the rap music blaring through the powerful speakers in the car. Through the windscreen he saw Bluebwai, his baseball-capped head bobbing furiously to the music. Fluxy shrugged his shoulders and continued over the pedestrian flyover on Bonsall Street. On the sloping wall leading down to the busy dual carriageway and above the rage of cars, someone had risked life and limb to paint a strange message:

WE GO AROUND IN THE NIGHT AND ARE CONSUMED BY FIRE.

For some reason the words haunted him. What did they mean? Were they some sort of omen? If so, for what? Why was he thinking about it anyway? He didn't fear those words. How could he? They were just words, probably painted by some druggie. Maybe even one of his own clients. The thought amused him and he smiled broadly, his gold tooth gleaming and the beat of the hardcore rap tune still thumping away in his head.

WE GO AROUND IN THE NIGHT AND ARE CONSUMED BY FIRE.

On the other side of the dual carriageway, he turned his head again for another proud look at his brand new, black Mercedes across the road. This was only the second time he'd driven it, and he was looking forward to making a long trip in it, maybe down to London or right across onto the continent. Maybe he would take his baby mother for a spin this weekend. He could surprise her and drive her to see her sister in Leeds. Yeah, he thought, that's what he would do this weekend. He felt a drop of rain fall on the tip of his nose and he glanced upwards to the sky which had become dark with clouds. It was going to rain.

Suddenly, from the corner of his eye, Fluxy saw a flash of blue and orange light accompanied by an explosion. For a fraction of a second his chest burned like it was on fire. In the next moment it seemed to disappear, as both barrels of a shotgun tore him to pieces. A short time later, Fluxy breathed his last gulps of air.

IT HAD BEEN a wicked experience. Storm sat silently in his late model BMW, looking out to sea, contemplating, his brow creased with anxiety, deep-set eyes watery, his lips dry and his soft, dark skin so taught around his face that the cleft on his chin seemed more pronounced than normal. Unusually for him, the stereo was turned down so low you could barely make out the soft melody of the lover's tune on the cassette.

Yes, it had been so moving and precious he didn't know whether to cry or shout with joy. And he'd been there, holding Lalah's hand as she sweated and pushed and screamed and pushed, until suddenly the baby's head appeared. The midwife cleared the baby's face and the rest of the tiny body followed. Storm was the father of a beautiful daughter. It had been a moving experience and something spiritual came over him, something he hadn't experienced for many years. Since, in fact, the Old Lady last dragged him to church. As far as he was concerned, Lalah was now his 'bonafide'.

There was nothing more he could do at St. Mary's hospital, they had said. The baby was rushed to the special care unit and that scared him. The doctors assured him that everything was satisfactory. Both mother and daughter were comfortable and doing fine, but they needed to rest. Storm left the hospital reluctantly, climbing into his car. The runnings he had to do that day now seemed insignificant. There were other things to consider. He had someone else to consider now. He switched off his mobile phone. He needed a moment's peace by himself to decide what he was going to do. He turned the ignition key and slipped the car into gear, then drove slowly out of the hospital car park, and just kept on driving.

He didn't know how he had got there, but he had joined the M62 and driven for about an hour, on the same road most of the way, until the road finally ran out on the Blackpool waterfront. He simply sat there, with the radio turned low. He didn't know how long.

Storm fiddled absent-mindedly with the diamond stud in his left ear. He was thinking big things. Thinking of all the things he had done wrong in his life which, back then, seemed alright. Thinking about his daughter and all the things he would do for her. She was born premature and weighed only four pounds. Lalah had called him on the mobile as she went into labour. He was in London, but cut his stay short to drive back to Manchester immediately. He arrived at the hospital just in time to be there with his woman.

His daughter was born with respiratory problems. They said it was a miracle the baby was alive. To Storm, it was not just a miracle, but a sign that she needed his love and attention. He would have to be extra-protective towards her. She would get everything, the most expensive clothes, the best education, and they would live in a nice house. He would send her to the best schools and she would be the prettiest girl as far as his eyes could see. What were they going to call her? The deal with Lalah was that he would get to name the child if it was a boy and she would get to name the child if it was a girl.

As he looked out to sea, he wished his car was a boat in which he could sail with his daughter over the oceans, beyond the horizon in the distance. He could take her away, far away from Manchester. They could escape to another land, another place. Or they could just keep sailing. He wouldn't have to keep looking over his shoulder on the high seas. Because out there he and his daughter would stand a better chance together. But who was he kidding? He plucked unconsciously at the hairs on his thin moustache and shook his head slightly trying to wash away his thoughts. The truth was that his baby daughter had inherited a father who juggled for a living and all he could do for her was his best. He looked at his watch and sighed. It was already after three in the afternoon. He must have been there for hours, but it seemed like minutes and now a slight drizzle had begun to fall. He glanced in his rearview mirror briefly. His face looked haggard and there were bags under his eyes. He needed to freshen up. He turned on the ignition and the engine roared into life. If the road was clear, he'd be able to make it back in time to go to his regular barbers for a shave and a haircut.

CHUCK D. THE lyricist of Public Enemy was rapping his way through *Fight The Power*, a classic tune with the youths. Bluebwai, his blue checkshirt unbuttoned to reveal a white singlet underneath, bobbed his head absent-mindedly to the tape, his foot tapping out a rhythm. Despite his light skin, blue eyes and curly dark-blonde hair, Bluebwai was black. And long before he identified himself solidly as so, police and the state had already 'tagged' him.

But that didn't bother him. In fact he was proud of it. He had suffered comments all through his life from both the black side of things, as well as the white side. Very early on, when it felt like he didn't fit anywhere, it hurt. For a time, he cursed the fact that he was 'in-between'. That was when he was younger. Things were different now. He knew he belonged. He was a Piper Mill man, a member of the crew, and for him that was like being part of the royal family.

As far back as he could remember, being a Piper Mill man was what he had always wanted. They'd been the neighbourhood crew for years and if you grew up in those few streets they controlled, it looked like the Piper Mill posse were the only ones who were having a good time. Blue was a smart kid and had done well in school, but all around him, everywhere he looked, he was bombarded with reminders of the materialistic world that didn't form part of his existence: the top-of-the-range sneakers, the expensive video games and the designer casual wear. Like many young kids his age, he wanted it all. He soon started figuring that he could sell drugs on the side, while still at school.

Blue started out as a scout for the massive. He was only thirteen, but owned a mountain bike, and that was all he needed to join the small army of junior G's. He acted as lookout for the posse, an early warning system to guard against surprise raids, not only from the cops. Every now and then an angry man would come looking for a soldier who had done him something, like taken his woman.

By the time he was fifteen, Blue was already pushing small quantities of mostly weed for the posse after school. Just recently, he got the chance to really impress the Piper Mill. The police had been chasing Jigsy one morning, lights flashing from behind. As Jigsy steered his ostentatious Jag around the corner, he threw a wrapped-up plastic bag out of the window. The police van came around the corner with a screech of tyres and continued their chase of the Jag. Fortunately, Blue was riding his mountain bike in the vicinity, on his way to sign on. He'd seen everything and quickly picked up the plastic bag before anyone saw him and tucked it under his jacket. When he managed to get far enough to deem it safe, he ducked into an alleyway and, for the first time, took a peep inside the plastic bag. From the moment he saw the small, neatly wrapped cellophane parcels inside, he knew what it was. And he knew what he had to do. He had to find Fluxy.

The social security officer didn't see him that morning. That was the morning Blue earned his colours and later that evening the entire Piper Mill welcomed him into the crew.

He sat listening to his music. Then suddenly, from the other side of the road, he heard an explosion which sounded like violent thunder. He looked up and only just saw Fluxy fall. All in the same movement, Bluebwai pulled the piece quickly from under the seat, jumped out of the Merc, and raced across the flyover. By the time he got to the other side, he was shaking and calling out Fluxy's name. Fluxy, lying on the ground, couldn't hear him. The sight of the shotgun's message froze Blue in his tracks. The chest wound was too big, and he'd lost too much blood for Fluxy to ever be able to hear anybody again. Fluxy was dead.

JIGSY, EASY-LOVE and Teeko sat in a corner of The Piper Mill Pub laughing and passing a spliff between them. On the table in front of them were their mobile phones and beepers, stacked in between drinking glasses and bottles of Dragon Stout and Pils.

From across the room, the pub's resident sound system pumped out heavy bass and drums, roots revival style. There weren't many people in the pub at this time of the day, so the greying rastaman behind the sound decks was happy to skank along with the music as he drew on a pungent stick of sensi.

The strong aroma of cannabis drifted out to Bedwell

Close and Quinney Crescent. This was the Alexandra Park housing estate in the heart of Moss Side. The fact that the Piper Mill headquarters was so close to Grange Close territory was an issue of contention between the two gangs and a surprise attack could not be ruled out. In the pub car park, young boys on mountain bikes roamed in the cold October air, calling out to each other, competing with each other and surveying their territory with an air of importance. Other boys held pit bull terrier dogs at their sides, with tight grips around their leashes. They were lookouts, paid to spot trouble, rival gangs or police. Some were brazen drug couriers, too young to be touched by the law.

The Piper Mill posse sat inside the smoky pub, laughing above the volume of the music from the sound system. Business was too good to mention. All they had to do was kick back and the dollars seemed to flow in. It was almost too good to be true. A trio of attractive girls by the bar gave them the eye. It wasn't unusual. Those who didn't know they were taxing the landlord assumed from their behaviour that they were running things in this particular public house.

Teeko, muscles bulging from under his black turtleneck pullover, his bald head glistening in the pub light, was counting a wad of money. A spliff bounced in his mouth, sparkling gold jewellery dangled from his thick neck and hands.

"Shit...," he lost count. "Whe' me deh? I can't concentrate on this with them girls watching," he muttered, shifting his beefy frame uneasily in his seat. Like most of his friends, he spoke in a mixture of Jamaican dialect and English, with a strong Manchester accent.

"What the fuck is wrong with you!" a red-eyed Jigsy yelled.

"Cool nuh, Jigsy."

"What the fuck are you doing!" Jigsy repeated. As always his head was covered in a bright-coloured bandanna, tightly-wrapped around his head like a turban. "That's our fucking money you're playing around with." In his brother's absence, he assumed leadership of the crew. Nobody disputed that.

Teeko's shaven head was light and he was in a playful mood.

"But the bitches..." he protested.

"Fuck them, T.K." Jigsy said.

"That's exactly what I intend to do," Teeko replied eagerly, his eyes wide. "All in a row."

"Keep your eyes on the money," said Jigsy. He wasn't in a jovial mood. An uneasy feeling had been clinging to him all day, like a swamp dragging him down. He hadn't seen or heard from his brother, Fluxy, since morning time, which was unusual. Fluxy should have been there by now. It wasn't like him to be late.

"Hey!" Teeko started to laugh, interrupting Jigsy's anxious thoughts. "We got big t'ings to celebrate. Big t'ings ah gwan 'bout yah! Not even beastbwai can test my man! 'Cause my man's comin' like the Moss Side Ninja — dem cyaan catch him!"

They all laughed, sharing the joke. Easy-Love raised his bottle of Dragon.

"To all informer man who waan distress we programme, we ah go shoot first, ask question later, seen!" Easy-Love, his funki dreds bouncing, announced to nobody in particular or whoever was listening.

Teeko and Jigsy drank to that. It had been a long day already, but Jigsy had beaten the rap. That was all that counted. Sitting in court, they heard the prosecutor ask Bow-Bow time and time again if Jigsy was the one who attempted to murder him. And they heard the short, but powerfully built, black youth repeatedly say no, he had never seen this man before in his life. The prosecutor couldn't believe it and in his upper class whine, reminded Bow-Bow of his signed statement saying that this was the man he'd picked out of an identity parade. He urged Bow-Bow to take a closer look. Bow-Bow took his time and stared at Jigsy closely, as if studying something in his eyes, then simply said, "I was mistaken. It wasn't him, I couldn't see so good, but I know it wasn't him."

Teeko and Easy saluted Jigsy for staying cool under pressure. He had done the posse proud. Something like this would serve as a warning to all the G's out there that Piper Mill fired strictly legal shots. Even beastbwai couldn't touch them.

Bow-Bow came from Cheetham Hill, a poor, run-down area, north of the city, predominantly populated by Asians and Blacks. From the poverty-ridden inner-city streets, a gang emerged, The Cheetham Panthers, who wanted to share the rich spoils of Moss Side, where people came from as far as Birmingham to purchase the best rock, hash or sensi.

It all happened the previous year. Bow-Bow hadn't reckoned with the full consequences of crossing Jigsy. As far as he was concerned, it was a straightforward robbery of a dealer. No big thing. An operation he'd performed several times before. An operation he carried out with increasing regularity. On Saturday nights he usually needed to get fucked up and robbing a dealer was always a guaranteed way of getting hooked up with supplies. If only he had chosen another dealer. This one seemed straightforward. He was sure the dealer was an independent. A youthful, small-time dealer no more than seventeen with a pock-marked, rugged face, in the passenger seat next to him, counting the money. It was all there. Next, the dealer lifted up his jacket, dipped his hand into his crutch and pulled out a small crumpled ball of tin foil. Bow-Bow unwrapped the tin foil slowly. He noticed the machete handle sticking out from the inside of the dealer's jacket, but he kept cool. Finally, he saw what he was looking for, the white magical rock in the centre of the foil.

"Good stuff," he nodded, as he tasted a few grains.

"Yeah man," the dealer said confidently. "Top stuff."

Before he knew it, the dealer was staring down the barrel of a deadly black revolver. Bow-Bow moved so fast, the dealer found himself trapped. He couldn't even pull out his chopper.

Bow-Bow smiled. He was getting more adept at this. He impressed himself with the speed and the fluidity of the stick-up. He was certainly improving.

"Gimme the fucking money back!" he barked.

The dealer obliged without hesitation, cold sweat forming a trickle on his brow.

"No problem, man," he urged, "tek it easy, seen. Tek all the money."

The dealer was a newcomer to the scene and didn't

know who the short man was, but he knew what the gun meant. It was only money. His life was worth more than that. But he couldn't understand who would be crazy enough to pull something like that on him. Even though he had only been operating a few weeks, most of the youths in the area knew that he had protection. Even people as far away as Cheetham Hill knew he was working for the Pipers. After Bow-Bow had driven off with his merchandise, the dealer called Jigsy on his mobile and gave him the registration number of the gunman's Volkswagen.

It wasn't until the early hours of the morning that one of the scouts called Jigsy's mobile from a pay phone. He had spotted the Golf GTi outside a blues dance in Cheetham Hill. If the call had come through for Fluxy, a decision would have been made calmly and collectedly. But Fluxy was out of town at the time, and Jigsy considered himself a bad motherfucker who allowed his anger to control his actions. Too bad for Bow-Bow. Jigsy and Teeko were waiting for him, parked across the road from the Golf, as he stepped out of the blues in the early hours of the morning.

Jigsy's eyes burned with rage when he saw the short man in the grey Trilby hat with the glamorous woman on his arm approach the car. So this was the motherfucker who'd crossed his territory and robbed his dealer. He reached for the baseball bat in the back seat and climbed quietly out of the Jag, followed by Teeko.

Bow-Bow had only just unlocked the passenger door for his date to climb into the stylish interior. He was buzzing, his mind racing, his eyes bulging. Nothing could be better. He walked across the front of the car to the driver's side and unlocked the door. He opened the door wide and was only partially inside the car, when the driver's door was given a hard push from the other side and slammed without mercy into Bow-Bow's elbow and knee.

The cry which screamed out of Bow-Bow came from somewhere deep down in his soul, somewhere so remote he didn't known it existed. The girl beside him screamed only once, before jumping out of the car to the safety of the street. The car door slammed repeatedly on Bow-Bow's knee, until finally Bow-Bow could scream no more, the echo of his voice dying in his throat. Finally the two men dragged him onto the road. While Teeko tested his new karate kicks on Bow-Bow as he lay on the ground, Jigsy swung wildly with the baseball bat, each strike accompanied by the sickening crack of bone breaking.

Somehow Bow-Bow survived, but he truly feared for his life after that. He had a cracked skull, cracked ribs, a smashed face and broken limbs and was in no doubt that his assailants would have killed him. The police interviewed him at the M.R.I. hospital when he was able to talk. He was reluctant to co-operate, but agreed with the officer when he stressed that the only way Bow-Bow could guarantee his own safety was to have his assailant locked up for good. It wasn't an easy decision for Bow-Bow. No Manchester posse member had ever done a deal with any police. Most would have dealt with the situation themselves. To deal with the police you were lower than a dog. Bow-Bow knew better. He knew that if he testified he would have to keep running. But if he didn't testify, Jigsy might finish the job off. There seemed to be no other choice but to accept the police's promise of complete anonymity until the trial and an undisclosed sum of money afterwards. Within days, the word got around that Bow-Bow had talked. By the time the trial came up, Bow-Bow had changed his mind. The Panthers had turned their backs on him, unable to believe that they had an informer in their midst. And Piper Mill got to him before he could testify. He had received a lock of his baby's hair with a threatening letter in the post. He didn't know how they got it and he didn't care. The message was clear. His woman and the youth were not safe. Fuck police protection, fuck it.

For the Piper Mill members in the pub, what mattered was that they controlled their area. They had maintained their legendary propensity for violence. Now everybody knew they would kill for their turf, or die for it, if they had to.

"Yuh cyaan touch dis," Jigsy said confidently, slapping his chest with a fist. "Don't worry about dat." He didn't fear any man, least of all police or society. He didn't fear God either. "Like I told the beastbwai dem, why don't you come work for me? I'll pay you double!"

Roaring and jeering contemptuously, the massive formed their fists and fingers into gang salutes.

"Any bwai try test we — dead!" Easy-Love promised, half-chanting. "An' dat goes for any man from Grange an' the rest ah dem batty bwai deh!"

More jeers and cheers of approval. Then, faintly below the roar of laughter, one of the mobile phones stacked up before them, began to ring softly. It was Easy's Nokia. He picked it up, still laughing.

18

"Yaow, dread at the controls," he answered.

Gradually the smile faded from his face.

"What happen, Easy?" Teeko asked him anxiously.

"Shush!" Easy urged, his hand trembling, a pained look on his face. "Who the hell is this? Bluebwai? Say that again... Who...? The fucking bastards, the fucking bastards...!!" Easy began to scream into his phone, everybody in the pub stopped what they were doing and looked over in his direction, nervously.

"The fucking bastards! We'll get them for this! Do you hear me?! We'll cut off their balls for this, the fuckkkkers!!!"

Easy-Love started to rise to his feet, and turned to his crew with cold, malevolent eyes, the phone slipping from his grasp.

"What is it? What is it, man? Tell us!" Jigsy urged, frozen in motion, his eyes burning.

Standing unsteadily, Easy-Love looked straight at Jigsy. "They got Fluxy," he said solemnly. "Fluxy's dead!!!" The entire pub fell silent. The customers were visibly shocked. Everybody knew Fluxy. Some had known him since he was just a little yout'man. From when he used to run errands for his mother in short pants. And that wasn't all that long ago. Could Fluxy really be dead?

"The bastards who pulled this must be crazy..." Easy-Love raged almost beside himself. "The fuckers...! The Grange fuckers...!!"

Jigsy said nothing. His eyes were wide, bloodshot and glazed and black bile rose in his throat and frothed at the corners of his mouth as he stared at the other members of his crew. Then his jaw dropped open slowly and a sound that started off as a whine from deep down in his stomach, slowly became a loud, piercing and haunting howl, like a man possessed.

ZUKIE RODE ALONG Moss Lane East. The squeaking red racer bike seemed to cut through the early morning traffic. The morning was grey and the cold wind blowing in his face, made his grey-green eyes watery and blew his sandy-coloured dreadlocks off his face.

A number 53 bus suddenly roared past him, a blur of orange and white too close for comfort, throwing him off balance. He uttered a strangled curse.

"Raas claat!"

The drizzle of rain didn't help his mood. Raising his head, Zukie glanced over at the dreary grey block of council flats in the distance. Empty, awaiting demolition. Row upon row, block upon block of solid, grimy, pigeon-shit concrete which made the area look bleak and cast a feeling of despair over those who lived nearby.

Moss Side was dry, he concluded, like the valley of dry bones in Ezekiel's vision in the Bible.

He turned right on to St. Mary's Street, where

21

Abasindi, the Black Women's Co-operative used to be based, in the old disintegrating church. A withered drunkard curled by and collapsed in the red, yellow and green doorway. He seemed oblivious to the cold, wet weather, oblivious to the world, comatosed by alcohol. Posters on the walls of the abandoned building advertised dance-hall sessions. One event stood out in particular for a forthcoming attraction, Shabba Ranks live at the Carib Club, admission £12.00, more on the door. It was a session he wanted to reach, somehow.

He continued peddling towards his destination, the new Job Centre building further up the road. He noticed the youths from a short distance away. He even recognised one or two of them, from when they used to live in the same neighbourhood, where you made your choices early. You either had to run with the posse or you were on your own. You also needed guts to stay in the gang. Zukie had guts, but preferred to use his brains. He wasn't interested in being 'the baddest bwai 'bout yah'.

The group of bandanna-wrapped, hooded, designer-leisure dressed youths gathered around a new registration, gleaming midnight-blue BMW, admiring its awesome volume of power. Seven, maybe eight of them stood staring lustfully. Somebody touched the boot spoiler. The car's super-sensory alarm system detonated itself immediately and the headlamps flashed on and off with the screaming horn. Its owner ran out of a shop. A pale white man, his face red, puffy and sweating. At the sight of the youths gathered around his pride and joy, he slowed down reluctantly.

Suddenly, somebody laughed.

"Yaow Tippa, how about this one?!" someone else called, his head half-hidden in a hooded sweatshirt, gold rope chains around his neck and rings on every finger.

The car owner moved closer towards his BM. With fumbling fingers, he pressed the remote control to deactivate the alarm and the automatic central locking system at the same time. He slipped into the car niftily, locking the doors behind him in the same movement. They were closing in on him. A look of terror came over his face as he slid the gear lever into reverse. The powerful vehicle seemed to leap backwards.

The youths leaped out of the way, just in time.

"We'll get you next time!" someone called after the hastily retreating BMW. Loud, arrogant laughter followed. The youths joked about the look on the white man's face and the odour of excrement that seemed to follow after him. One of them pulled out a wad of notes and started counting. There must have been a thousand pounds there. Satisfied, he stuffed the notes into a leather pouch around his waist.

Sitting at a standstill on his bike, Zukie watched and listened. He smiled to himself when he thought of the irony of building the new Job Centre opposite the probation offices on Chichester Road. An olive-skinned, male vagrant, smelling strongly of beer and wearing a shabby coat, clattered his way past. Muttering incessantly to himself, he raised a battered food flask above his woolly, uncombed head, looking up towards the grey sky. He shook the flask, performing some sort of ceremony, his eyes half-closed and lifeless. The man was in limbo, neither dead nor alive, neither asleep nor awake. Twenty-one years old, a hostage to crack.

Zukie glanced over at the two approaching youths and recognised them instantly as his close friends Hair Oil and Chico. Chico was about half a head taller than the other, with a dark complexion and a mane of untidy, shoulder-length dreadlocks. His matted hair stuck out at all angles from under a huge tam. The smaller youth, Hair Oil, was brown-complexioned, a few freckles interspersed on his face. His dreadlocks were short, thin, tidy and neat.

"Zukie!" Chico called, grinning from ear to ear, "Boo-yah! What happen, Blood?"

"Huh?!!"

"Jeeze, look how long I been calling you. Looks like yuh been fading out."

They punched a fist salute. Then Zukie touched Hair Oil's fist lightly with his own.

"Jeezas, Oil, look 'pon him nuh," Chico teased. "Him saddle up 'pon bicycle an' t'ing!"

Zukie merely smiled. Chico and Hair Oil were his bredrin, rasta culture-wise and otherwise. And he didn't mind sharing a joke with them. They probably realised that the second-hand bike cost Zukie most of his savings, but that was cool. He needed his iron horse, without it he was lost, trapped in Hulme, at the Old Lady's house, his feet, his only other carriage.

"Yes, so yuh a big timer now," Hair Oil added, giving the bike the once over with overstated admiration.

The atmosphere between them was convivial as they teased each other.

"Well," Zukie started to say, drawing the word out of his mouth slowly so that it had the desired effect, "times

24

are really hard now. Man cyaan even afford a five pound spliff."

Chico whistled a sigh, nodding over at the gang of smartly dressed youths, mobile telephones in their back pockets. "They got it made," he said, "good clothes, cars, women galore. All they got to do is stand 'pon street corner and hustle."

"Yeah," Hair Oil reasoned, twisting one of the baby locks on his head out of habit. "I like the things money can buy, but I in't gonna kill for it. Nah man!! I mean, look what went down last night. It's like a fuckin' war. I'm too young to die. I'm better off shacking up at my mum's. She got plenty food, plenty love, plenty money. I don't need the bad bwai business, fe real. You always have to be sneaky with drugs because you know how much you're hurting your community, man. I don't wanna live like that, man."

Zukie changed the subject. "Unuh fin' work yet?"

"Work?" Chico asked in disgust, his shiny black face screwing up tightly, his mouth spreading wide. He exploded into husky, deep and violent laughter. "Work?! Where? Here? Joke you a joke, man!"

Zukie felt slightly despondent. They were all eighteen and Chico hadn't had a proper job since leaving school with good GCSE results. Still, Zukie tried to be positive. He was strong and believed that one day he'd find a decent job.

With Zukie and his friends, every discussion ultimately came around to women. In this case, the beautiful, brown-skinned girl with long curly hair in the passenger seat of a passing car. Zukie vaguely recognised her, but he couldn't remember where from.

25

The girl tossed her head around briefly as the car drove by and just for a moment parted her cherry-red painted lips. She smiled playfully at Zukie and winked, before turning her head round.

Chico stood there drooling, hungering to savour a taste. He tried to call after her, but the car accelerated away. Chico sighed regretfully.

"Who was that?" Zukie asked, easing the bike forward again.

"Didn't you recognise her? Paradise Browne, Pastor Browne's daughter. And that was her mum driving. Yuh 'member?"

Zukie remembered. But he hadn't remembered her looking like that!

"Now dat gyal can come powder me any day," Hair Oil insisted.

"Cho' man," Chico said, "she wouldn't give you the time of day."

"What do you mean?"

"Didn't you see how she couldn't take her eyes off of *me*?"

"Yuh mad! Either that or all that wanking is making you short-sighted."

Hair Oil had gone too far, Chico felt.

"I don't deal with them kinda t'ings. Me have 'nuff woman..."

"Do you have to talk about her like that?" Zukie cut in.

"Aaaah?! So what's all this?" Chico asked. "It seems like young Zukie want Paradise fe himself!"

Zukie shrugged his shoulders. "Not really. Yuh cyan just talk about the preacher's daughter dem way deh."

His friends teased Zukie some more. He wasn't being completely frank. After a few more minutes of chat, Chico and Hair Oil took their leave. They had runnings to attend to. Zukie watched them dip and duck recklessly across the road. He saw a blue Jag pull up to them and after a moment, he saw them climb in. As the car screeched away hurriedly, Zukie wondered who Chico or Hair Oil knew who had that kind of dollars.

Zukie pedalled on. The area had once been a busy shopping area, but many of the shops had closed down. Even the shopping centre had been raised to the ground after years of decay and crime. Some said it was the recession, but that couldn't be. Zukie often thought about it and always concluded that there was enough money in the area to have kept the shopping centre bustling and enough people willing to spend their money.

Zukie finally arrived at the Job Centre on Moss Lane East. Zukie leaned the bike up against the wall and stepped inside. Chico is right, he thought, glancing around the spartan Centre, what the hell am I going to find in here? Sighing deeply, he took two strides forward and stood in front of the display board. Only slave wages were on offer. Still, he scanned each display card with hope, followed by trepidation, then disappointment. The words, 'EXPERIENCE NECESSARY' jumped out of every card. He noticed the two dark-skinned girls, one with a bob wig and psychedelic lycra leggings, the other with long curly permed hair and wearing a green mini skirt, watching him. He gave them an uncertain smile. They began to giggle. His face flushed like hot fire. Without realising

27

it, he had taken one of the cards from the board in front of him:

NO EXPERIENCE NECESSARY.

Required immediately, smart, young worker for general maintenance in a busy bingo hall. Must have pleasant, outgoing personality, must be able to paint and decorate to a high standard. Should be able to do some joinery and basic electrics. Must have relevant certificates. Training where necessary.

DAY RELEASE for suitable candidate. WAGES £120.00 per week, excluding Saturday and bonus.

His eyes remained glued to the salary. Backing away towards the assistants, he sat down and waited. Eventually a pale, red-headed woman turned to him.

"How may I help you?"

Zukie stared at her for a few seconds, as she nervously adjusted her large square spectacles on the edge of her shiny nose. He sat there lost in thought. Breathing deeply, he eventually passed the card to her.

"You're not supposed to take the card off the board," she said, her voice betraying more than a hint of agitation. This was no laughing matter.

"I know, I forgot."

"Anyway," she continued, without raising her head to look at him, "this vacancy has been filled. The notice shouldn't have been up. Two hundred applicants applied."

HE HAD LOST his brother only the previous day, but Jigsy thought he could take it like a man. Yet seeing his heart-broken mother, quietly going mad over the news of the death of her son, brought tears to his eyes.

He told her the evening before, a few hours after Blue's call came through. He had to tell her. He hadn't wanted her to hear it from the police or anyone else. He hadn't wanted to have to tell her himself either. But that was the only way he could guarantee to be there with her, to give her support, when she heard.

"Mum!" he called as he rushed through the front door of his mother's flat. His heart was pumping and his breath was quickening. "Mum!" he called again, this time more urgently. But she wasn't in the living room and she wasn't in the kitchen. By now, tears filled Jigsy's eyes. He was in a panic. The sudden realisation of what he was about to say stunned him. "Mum!" he called out one more desperate time, "Mum, Glenn's dead!"

His mother rushed out of her bedroom, still slightly dazed from her sleep, to meet him in the hallway. She simply stared at her turbaned son, shaking her head slowly, refusing to accept what he was saying.

"Mum! Mum!! He's dead. Glenn, he's dead!" Jigsy sobbed, shedding tears for his mother, for his brother and for himself. "He's dead!" Jigsy's sobbing seemed to have little impact on his mother. He wanted her to open her arms wide for him to bury his head in her bosom while he cried, but she still refused to believe what she heard. Her tiny frame seemed not to be able to withstand such an impact. How could Glenn be dead? How could my son be dead? He is only 21, just a baby. And he is strong and healthy. He has never been sick.

29

How could he not be alive? That's not how it's supposed to be. A mother is supposed to die before her baby, how could it be any other way? Why was Marvin lying to her?

Jigsy was still not fully recovered when Bluebwai returned to the Piper Mill pub to confirm the news he had earlier phoned through. He was still shaken up, but made it back to base, driving Fluxy's Merc like crazy to get away from the scene of the murder before the cops came. He had never witnessed a killing before and he still felt like retching.

Jigsy made Bluebwai go through every detail. Why wasn't he covering Fluxy? Where did the shot come from? Was he sure that Fluxy was dead? How could he be sure? Bluebwai assured him time and time again that he knew he was certainly dead.

"I don't fuckin' know how I know he was dead, Jigs. You just fuckin' know, that's how. You just fucking know..."

The youth was too choked to carry on. Jigsy didn't even know why he was asking all the questions, didn't care what the answers were, his mind was all confused and his heart was racing away at a furious pace and he didn't know what he was going to do first, second or last. Easy-Love and Teeko tried to calm him down, but it was no use. Easy offered him a spliff, but Jigsy was too shaky to smoke it. Finally, he decided it was time to drive to his mother's flat. He stepped outside and climbed in the Jag, his eyes wild with terror. Fiddling around with the ignition keys, he turned the motor, then slipped it into gear and pointed it in the right direction.

Even though her sons often offered to move her to a

30

home in a more salubrious location, Mrs Ellis chose to stay on the Alexandra Park Estate in the heart of Moss Side. Even after her sons moved into an exclusive address, she preferred to stay in the area where all her friends were, that she was familiar with. She was too old to be changing address, she had said. She only intended to be moving one more time in this life and that was to go back home, lock, stock and barrel.

It was to this old family home that Jigsy returned to inform his mother of her eldest son's death. The enormity of what he was about to do didn't fully hit him until he was only a few yards from his mother's blue-painted front door. That's when his feet began to feel like lead and they seemed to drag the last few steps. He had saved his tears until he got home, saved his emotions until he told his mother. But now he was there, she refused to believe what he told her.

THE FRONT DOOR slammed fiercely and the Old Lady staggered into the living room, having returned from work with two heavy carrier bags in each hand. She called out for Zukie, but there was no sound from upstairs.

She laid the bags to rest on the worn carpet in heaps. The living room was large and sombre with an abundance of ornaments and furniture. The walls were adorned with family portraits and religious prints depicting Christ, with open arms, bleeding and the Last Supper. The Old Lady called out for Zukie again. Still

31

no reply. She kissed her teeth and sat down.

Still seated, she struggled out of her coat, laying it carefully on the back of the armchair. She was worn out after a hard day at work and shopping. The Old Lady wriggled out of her small heeled shoes and soothed her broad feet with a caressing hand. Her toes were frozen numb.

"Wish I did come to this country and learn somet'ing... Coulda been a doctor..." she wheezed, looking round the room. "Or somet'ing."

She called for her son again. Still nothing stirred in the house. Too exhausted to lift her heavy frame to look for him upstairs, she remained seated, catching her breath. Everybody had told her to lose weight, the doctors, her sons, and everybody else she knew. But that was easier said than done. If they had gone through one tenth of the tribulation she had gone through in recent years, they too would have ballooned in size, they too would have turned grey. England was a bitch which had knocked some of the fight out of her, but not her spirit. She rarely smiled nowadays, but when she did, the smile would reveal that same gap between her front teeth which in her younger days was often how people identified her. Her eye caught the school photograph of her son on the wall, taken before he grew dreadlocks. Why did Zukie have to resemble his father so closely? Why couldn't he favour her like his brother Clifton? Not a day passed without her immediately thinking of Vermont when she saw her son. And that made her angry. It reminded her of all the hate she felt for her husband. And because Vermont wasn't around, she took her hate out on the person who most resembled him —

Zukie. Seeing Zukie's photograph now made her think of Vermont, wherever he was, once again.

"Vermont don't even know seh Zuchael exist," she muttered to herself. "Couldn't care less if he did. Bwai look just like him too. Same face, same greyish yeye. The bwai was just formin' in me belly. Gone. Never look back since. Eighteen years ago..."

The Old Lady's temper burned as she relived old, painful memories.

"Vermont probably livin' up in style. But not a penny him send fe the pickney..."

There was a pause in the Old Lady's thoughts. She heard the front door close gently. A huge smile spread across her face as Clifton entered the living room, to the surprise of his mother. "Cliff, Clifton!" Here was her favourite son, the son that had made something of his life, the son she could be proud of. The son that took after her.

Clifton smiled back, took off his designer sunglasses, his arms open wide to embrace her. His hair was close shaven, with a sharp parting cut into the left side. He was dressed in a parka type black leather jacket, underneath it a brown and red silk shirt with baggy, Karl Kani denim jeans and a pair of top class Timberland boots. He was tall and broad-shouldered and much darker in complexion than his younger brother.

"Wha'ppen Mummy?" he announced, grinning. "Long time, no see."

The Old Lady rushed towards him, her arms extended. His words were lost in her bosom as she embraced him heartily. "Clifton is where yuh been so

33

long? Lawd me son, mek me look 'pon you!! Yuh look good. What ah way yuh clothes them posh," she said proudly.

She was full of admiration for her son, who was exceptionally handsome, with evenly shaped features, thick sensual lips, and a square jaw with a cleft dividing his chin. He was not only powerfully built, but had a good job and earned a decent living. The Old Lady always felt secure with him around. The only thing she didn't like was that he still wore an earring in his left ear. But she wasn't going to chastise him about it now. She was so happy he had come home.

"So how long yuh stayin' for?" she asked him nervously, afraid that as easily as her joy had come, it could be taken away.

"Don't worry Mum," Clifton assured her, "I'll be here a few days."

IT WAS LATE evening and they had been driving around in the heavy rain for a couple of hours with no particular place to go. Windscreen wipers switching in double time, Easy-Love steered the BMW effortlessly from street to street and area to area, cutting into smaller roads and then turning back on the busy streets. Teeko next to him was operating the sounds, ejecting one cassette and inserting another. Nothing he played seem to suit their gloomy mood. In the back seat, Bluebwai stared out of the window with a blank expression on his face. He was over the shock, but was still taking Fluxy's killing badly. Too badly for Easy-Love's comfort.

"Don't worry, Blue" he assured the young soldier, glancing back at him in the rear view mirror, "we'll get those bastards. Don't worry about a thing. And when we drop the payback, you in't gonna feel so bad anymore. Trust me."

From the back seat, Bluebwai could just make out Easy's reassuring face glancing up at the rearview mirror back at him. He smiled, a smile that said nothing we do can bring Fluxy back.

Easy gunned the motor of the BMW and headed towards the bright lights of the City Centre. He didn't know why. They were killing time, waiting for something to happen. They didn't know exactly what would happen, but they were prepared for any eventuality.

"Bwoy, I couldn't be responsible for my actions if we bucked up on a Grange bwai right now."

Teeko grinned.

"I know what you're saying." He cocked up his fingers like a pistol and made a 'boom' sound with his mouth. "They won't have to come looking for me, 'cause I'll be ready and waiting when they are."

The music played at low volume. Easy was driving at a cruise speed, yet he was unable to ease the tension building up inside himself. Despite their bold words, neither Easy nor Teeko underestimated the task at hand. Taking on the Grange wouldn't be easy. Neither of them paused to contemplate that going head on against the Grange, they were risking their own lives as well. Shit no. That kind of thing happened to other people. Fluxy was just unlucky, that was all. Just fucking unlucky. Shit like that wasn't going to happen to them though. They had their firepower and they weren't exactly in the habit of praying that they would have no use for it.

"Even if one of the fuckers so much as looks in my direction," Teeko promised, running a hand confidently across his smooth scalp, "he's dead. I in't taking nothing from none of them."

Easy agreed. All the hanging around was making him twitchy. The only problem was that they were under strength. With Fluxy gone, they had also lost Jigsy temporarily. That was understandable. He was with his mother. He had to do his grieving. But to take on the Grange, they would need the entire posse. Earlier, Teeko had taken Blue and Easy down to the gym for a workout. When you were going into battle you had to make sure that every part of you was fit and ready, Teeko had said. And he was right, after all Bruce Lee always did. Easy felt hyped up and ready for anything. Every muscle in his body was tense and capable of doing anything. What's more, the tone-up had improved his looks. His muscles bulged slightly beneath his shirt, and that was good news.

THE OLD LADY turned over in her huge bed. She was perspiring heavily and wheezing as she slept. Her eyes flickered from side to side behind her closed lids. She was dreaming, a vivid nightmare.

She was lying in a coffin. It was cold, dark and her

breath was being squeezed out of her lungs. How long had she been under? Down here? How long? Her fingers passed over the silk material covering the sides. Tears fell from the corners of her eyes. She was being buried alive.

Zukie was burying her. She knew it was him. Sometimes he cried like a child, sometimes he just laughed. She could hear him hastily shovelling dry earth down upon her casket.

She started to twist and turn, struggling in vain. Kicking and striking the lid of the coffin with her fists. She begged Zukie for forgiveness. All she heard from him was demented laughter, and the sound of the shovelled earth crashing on to the lid of the casket.

The Old Lady woke up, wet with perspiration. Sitting up, she quickly untangled herself. She sat upright and looked around the room. Her eyes scanned the overcrowded dressing table, the overfull wardrobe, the two navy blue trunks that came over with her from Jamaica over twenty years ago. The Old Lady felt edgy and sick. Why could she not love Zukie as much as she loved Clifton? She reached for her inhaler on the bedroom table and inhaled a couple of short blasts.

ONCE AGAIN THE coconut shell chalice passed to Zukie on his right hand side. His head was already swimming and his body charged, but he took the pipe respectfully and pulled a long, hard draw that set the herb burning in a red flame at the bottom. He passed the chalice on, holding the smoke down for as long as he could, feeling the rush to his head and the blood in his eye. he was under the sensi.

"Yout'..." Zukie felt a hand touch his arm gently. He looked up and saw Brother Zeb, the rasta elder with the knotted, greying beard, smiling kindly at him. "Whatever you do in life, just try a little harder to mek it in this white man's world, just to say you did it."

Brother Zeb disappeared in a cloud of smoke leaving his words hanging. Zukie tried to focus. It was midnight. He was in his former junior school, sitting in the old assembly hall where he used to stand in the mornings along with everyone else, dressed in his school uniform and short trousers, saying the Lord's Prayer off by heart without understanding what it all meant. Now, the assembly hall was filled with smoke, the smoke from the sacred herb, as found on King Solomon's grave over two thousand years before, a tradition The Rasses were determined to continue.

The Old Lady moved to Hulme before the school closed down and became a rehearsal studio for local bands. But it still seemed strange to Zukie to be sitting in the middle of his old assembly hall burning the chalice. Back in the day, the headmaster would have whacked you for talking in assembly, let alone smoking some sensi.

The chalice done, someone shouted out "Jah!", which the others present followed immediately by the reply "Rastafari!" and the drumming started again. The Rasses always dressed in long red, green and gold robes, with their locks wrapped in matching headwear or impossibly concealed in African pill box hats. They were a local troupe of musicians, drummers and dancers who performed the living tradition of African music with strictly conscious tunes, accompanied by some serious kente drumming. Zukie laid his head back on the floor, facing the ceiling and listened to the spiritual music coming at him in voice and drum chants, hymn-like music similar to the hymns he had heard when his devout church-going mother used to drag him with her to the House of Worship. And while Zukie listened, his mind drifted off, far away, far, far away, to the land of his dreams, Africa. He didn't care where, but somewhere he could live up in the hills surrounded by the beauty of God's world, living clean and uncorrupted, eating fresh fish and fresh fruit, living simply but sufficiently. Some place he could meditate and elevate himself into the man that was lurking within him. A place where he could farm a couple of acres to make himself self-sufficient. Where there were no drugs and no gangs and no police and no bad bwais. A place where people just lived good amongst each other, and helped each other, and woke up every morning happy to see each other. And there, over the hills and across the valleys, where he would find his resting place, was where he would start his family. Thoughts of Paradise flooded back to him, as they had done several times since he saw her pass by briefly the day before. In his mind, she was there with him in his garden of Eden. She was his wife, the mother of his children, and they lived happily ever after. As Zukie lost himself in those sweet thoughts, The Rasses continued chanting and drumming as they had done since early afternoon:

Run come rally rally round
Come rally rally round
Jahovia's throne...
Come away, run away, come away from
Sodom and gommorah
Run away, come away from the land of the
sinking sand

I N HIS DREAMS it was an ambush in the night.
Every weapon was aimed at him. Clifton
screamed. Then he opened his eyes and sat
straight up. He looked around him. He was in bed,
terrified. The sheets were drenched with perspiration.
Sweat poured down his face. His heart pounded triple
time. He felt an insect crawling along his arm. He
looked down, observing it silently for a few seconds.
Then he flattened it with the palm of a shaky hand...

Outside, it was raining heavily. Clifton was
perspiring all over, having woken up abruptly. It was
morning, but it felt like he hadn't slept at all. He now sat
on the edge of the double bed, his head in his hands,
attempting to block out the nightmare still vivid inside
his head.

It wasn't the first interrupted sleep he'd had, in fact it
was becoming the norm. He dreaded night time because
he knew he must sleep sometime, yet all he had waiting
for him were nightmares. However strong and tough
and clever he was, he couldn't escape them.

He took a drag from his first cigarette of the day. One smoke a day had turned into one pack a day, and one pack a day had almost become two packs.

He took his mobile out of the charger and dialled the hospital. Mother and child were in good condition said the nurse. But they wanted to keep them in for a day or two to do a few tests on the premature baby. It was nothing to worry about.

Clifton snapped the phone shut. He lit another cigarette out of desperation, frustration, hopelessness, fear. He blew out a cloud of smoke and stared into empty space. All he saw before him was darkness and death. No not death, his mind cried. His woman, Lalah, had brought new life into the world. He had been there. The life of his little daughter was part of him.

He thought about the last few weeks he had spent in London, getting to know the scene down there and hooking up with one or two suppliers. He missed the fullness of London. It was the discreetness he liked, the way the big city swallowed you up. Not like Manchester where people knew you were in town before you touched down on Moss Side turf.

The mobile phone rang. It was Lewty, a close friend and loyal soldier, checking in early.

"Yaow homie!" His friend's voice cried down the phone, "where you been? I been calling you for days Storm."

"Yeah, yeah, yeah!" Clifton replied. "The mobile wasn't working," he lied. "But it's sorted now. So, waddap?"

"You heard about Fluxy?"

Clifton's ears pricked up. "What about him?"

"You in't heard about it! You must have been on Mars or sump'n man. Everybody knows this shit."

Finally Clifton managed to get the story from Lewty, the little he knew. Shit! Clifton couldn't believe it. Fluxy, dead! Despite the Grange's frequent runnings with Piper Mill, Fluxy was a man Clifton held a grudging respect for. They had known each other in passing for years though never previously held any particular liking or dislike for each other. They had just seen each other around a lot, and acknowledged the fact with a nod of the head every now and then. But the past six months had seen an increasing tension between the two crews. Sometimes, their business activities overlapped and that meant that somebody would have to back down. That was the problem. Because backing down meant losing respect, and if you lost respect you may as well call it a day and go looking for handouts. But now Fluxy was dead. Lewty only had sketchy details of what went down and no word on the perpetrators, but somehow Clifton knew that Fluxy's death was really bad news.

Clifton felt his stomach twist with fear. He needed something to relax him. He pulled his little brown leather pouch from under the pillow and built a spliff. As he smoked it, his mind began rising steadily. The room floated. His thoughts drifted to his successes. How he had built his crew up to the point where they were one of the most effective posses in Manchester. He had planned their ascent meticulously, merging with other crews when necessary and swallowing up the small time operator. There was no longer any unauthorised dealing on Grange turf, but he still didn't have time to sit back and cruise or relax, because it was to him that everyone turned. He was always under pressure, always looking over his shoulder. Remembering the responsibility that his mother instilled in him in childhood, he set the highest goals for himself and often dreamed about controlling the merchandise in the whole of Manchester. One day. But that wasn't what he wanted anymore. What kind of ambition was that? Thoughts of his little daughter clung to him. If Fluxy got hit, so could he. What would happen to his baby then?

Wrapping a towel around his nakedness, he headed downstairs to the bathroom for a long, hot, relaxing bath. He was home now, for a while. The Old Lady's house would be a good place to lie low and at the same time, he would be able to spend some time with her, like she was always asking him to. Nobody would think of looking for him here. And if this thing blew out of proportion, he would need to lie low.

From the kitchen, the exotic smell of a Caribbean breakfast of dumplings, saltfish and callaloo wafted out. Even though it was Saturday, the Old Lady, as usual, was up early. She didn't mind cooking for Clifton. In fact, she insisted on it, confident that if all else failed, the taste of some good home cooking would keep her son home, permanently.

"Look how me make yuh dumplin's dem fresh and crispy. Me know how much yuh love dem too," she said, when Clifton eventually appeared for his breakfast.

She placed the hot plate of culinary delicacies in front of him and waited as he wolfed down the meal. Eventually, she asked him the question that had been on her mind.

44

"Clifton where yuh been? Where you keep disappearing to fe such a long while?"

He took a long sip of hot coffee. It seemed like a long time before he answered, with a sigh.

"Mum, you know my job. I'm a salesman. I have to travel a lot."

"So you can't write or phone?"

Clifton sipped at his coffee.

"I'm sorry, Mum. I forgot. I'm always under pressure. I just can't afford to lose my job. You know how dread it is to find a decent job out there. I'm doing it for you. All of this. To make it easier for you. It's my turn to take care of you."

The Old Lady winced. She smiled painfully, unease eating away inside her.

"Jasmine comes around," she began to say awkwardly, "quite often, wid Lee."

Clifton said nothing. He didn't like to be reminded of Jazz. There was nothing he could do about the kid either. She had him and didn't want his father around. He would explain to Lee when he was old enough to know, that whatever else his mother told him, his father had always been there for him.

"Clifton, you have to go and see her. She's on her own round there. Can't be easy. She worried all the time."

"What she have to be worried about?" He sucked through his teeth harshly.

"Clifton, me don't care how much woman you have, or how much baby mother you have. That a fe yuh business. But you know that girl isn't use to that sort of life. She might put on a bright face, but she deserve bettah!"

45

For some reason Clifton laughed. He thought about letting the Old Lady know she now had a granddaughter as well, but he decided that this was probably not the best time.

The Old Lady smiled a nervous smile. "Think about it," she said.

Clifton shivered.

THE RAIN HAD stopped falling heavily. It turned instead into a delicate drizzle. A police car screamed past and faded somewhere into the distance, shooting red and blue lights into the early Saturday morning.

Zukie glided on the old bicycle, aimlessly cruising out of the Alexandra Park Estate, leaving the blues and shebeens behind him, leaving the early morning drug-pushers in doorways, like scavenger birds waiting for their prey.

Riding out of the huge estate of avenues and walks, he cycled past Grange Close and Bedwell Close. The Piper Mill pub wasn't far off, but he wanted to avoid the gang territories. He rode down Claremont Road, towards Alexandra Road South, towards the area of Whalley Range. This particular area of Whalley Range was notorious for prostitutes and when a couple of them looking for late business viewed him, they knew his was a poor prospect. Whalley Range was also where Paradise Browne lived.

"Pastor Browne house," Zukie said aloud. He wondered how he had ended up here, of all places.

Ahead of him, his breath formed in waves in the cold air. He heard his stomach rumble heavily. He was hungry, cold and wet. His head began to throb. The start of a migraine. Zukie felt sick and dizzy.

With numb shaking hands he lit, after the fourth attempt, his last cigarette from a packet from his leather jacket pocket. Curling his fingers around the naked flame of his plastic lighter to warm himself up.

After a moment, the tapping registered in his brain. Someone was trying to attract his attention from the upstairs window. His eyes strained up to the see the figure beckoning. Hesitantly, he glanced over his shoulder. Checking. There was no one about. He swallowed cold, dry air. His feet moved in a steady walk towards the house.

He opened the gates and entered the front garden. The bare trees looked ominous in the early morning. He remembered this garden and how, when he was younger, it seemed so big. He remembered thinking as a child that it was the Garden of Eden. The fountain, the flowers, the birds in summer...

As he walked up the gravel to the house he heard a soft growl and became aware of two hungry-looking rottweillers watching him carefully. Shit, Pastor was taking no chances, he reflected quickly. Zukie halted in his tracks. The two dogs looked well maaga, but fortunately they were chained. He gave them a wide berth, unwilling to turn around in case they jumped up and bit him.

The window above opened, splitting into two open frames.

"Zuchael?" A soft, female voice, tinged with a gentle

urgency, called him. He recognised it. "It's me, Paradise. From Sunday School class. Remember?"

Zukie remembered. He remembered the Old Lady dragging him along to church every Sunday. He remembered her slapping him for not reading his Bible, then hitting him again for crying. He was there specifically to remember. And maybe get a glimpse of Paradise, the brown-skinned beauty. It had been so long and she had previously worn horn-rimmed spectacles and her hair in plaits.

"Say something then," a giggly voice shouted through the open window. Zukie looked around nervously. Unwilling to encounter the wrath of waking her father up, he whispered loud enough for her to hear:

"Long time no see, Paradise."

"So are you going to stand there all day?" she asked.

Zukie looked about him nervously. It didn't sound like she was sending him on his way, but she couldn't seriously be suggesting that he come in. Her strict father would kill him for less. He saw something fall from Paradise's fingers, dropping to the frozen lawn below the window. The soft tinkle of keys.

"Let yourself in," she said pointedly. She seemed to read his thoughts exactly. "Don't worry, there's nobody here but me."

Zukie didn't need any more encouragement and quickly entered the house.

Paradise was waiting for him in the hallway. Zukie stood by the front door, a nervous smile edging across his face. He stared at her. She stared right back at him. She laughed. He laughed too. As if for the first time, he saw Paradise Browne in all her beauty. She really was beautiful. Brown-skinned, neither dark nor light, but what some people call "in between colour". She had round, dark brown eyes, a full top lip, a fine nose and long, curly hair. Her features arrested him. Through her flimsy, white cotton dress he could make out the visible form of her body.

Paradise observed him closely. Taking the keys gently from his cold hand, she led him, grinning, her eyes twinkling wickedly, towards the living room.

"I love the dreadlocks," she said with a big smile. She also had her memories of Zukie and in those days, he only had one hair style, which was a short back and sides and all over.

The thought crossed Zukie's mind that she was a little too inviting, but he quickly remembered that this was Paradise Browne, the pastor's daughter. Her smile was simply polite and friendly, he convinced himself. He was here to talk, nothing more. Besides Zukie wasn't the type to disrespect women. Suddenly he remembered something. "My bike, it's in the garden, some one might see it," he said anxiously.

"Why are you whispering?" Paradise asked. "Nobody's here. Everybody's gone to a church convention in Birmingham for the weekend."

Zukie let out a sigh of relief. Everything seemed to be working out nicely. He still couldn't believe that this was the same polite and quiet, bespectacled girl who, back in the day, used to sit quietly in church. But he felt more relaxed now he knew her father wasn't at home.

THE OLD LADY was thinking herself lucky for not having to go to work today. She stood next to the kitchen sink, watching the rain fall against the window pane. It had rained on the day of her wedding to Vermont too. Old time Jamaican people had a saying: if it rained on your wedding day, your marriage would be a disaster. Vermont. Vermont, who made her laugh, who made her feel important and beautiful. Vermont who also made her cry. He was as unpredictable as the sun and the rain. There could be no other like him for her. No one.

The house was like an empty shell of bricks and mortar. Funny how she missed her sons when they weren't there. She sighed. Rainy days always had this effect on her. She hoped Clifton would be home soon. She would make a nice soup for him. His favourite pumpkin soup. And where was Zukie? He hadn't been home all night. Why couldn't he let her know where he was going? Didn't he realise that she would be worried about him, with the streets as violent as they are? Closing her eyes in an attempt to stop the panic rising, she counted backwards from a hundred slowly.

The knocking at the front door brought her back to the here and now. The Old Lady swung her aproned body around quickly and went to see who it was. Glancing in the hall mirror on her way, she wiped her hands on the front of the floral apron and then looked through the glass spy hole.

A middle-aged white woman stood on the doorstep, looking around agitatedly. Puzzled, the Old Lady opened the door slightly, giving herself enough space to poke her head through. "Yes?" she asked abruptly. "Can

I help you?"

"I'm looking for Mrs Henrietta Delaphene Michaels."

There was no mistaking the strong Jamaican accent. For a moment the Old Lady was locked into the grey-eyed stare. She looked at the freckled skin, but she wasn't entirely sure. Something inside her refused to admit or to believe. Suddenly her heart was racing.

"I am she," the Old Lady answered hesitantly. "Who is enquiring?"

After a pause the other woman said, "Imelda Michaels. Hello, Queenie, long time, no see. I didn't even recognise you. You've changed so much."

"Imelda." The whispered name bounced off the Old Lady's quivering lips.

"Nuh tell me seh, you nuh recognise yuh husband sister!"

Silence. Then, "It's been a long, long time," the Old Lady said solemnly. "What mek me graced with your presence?"

"I've come to build some bridges."

"I didn't burn any bridge," the Old Lady said bitterly.

"Queenie, we all ah we, burn the bridges. Is what happen, yuh nuh tek me off yuh wet doorstep?"

The Old Lady hadn't seen Imelda for so many years, she wasn't sure if she wanted to see her now.

"How you know me live here?" the Old Lady asked suspiciously.

"A friend of a friend," came Imelda's reply.

The Old Lady watched Imelda's eyes darken, then look away, as Zukie would, as Vermont did, when they lied.

"Please, please Queenie, let me in."

51

The Old Lady sighed frustratingly, wanting to scream, why should I? Why should I let you inna me house? What have you ever done for me? Instead she said calmly, "Come in."

Indoors by the gas fire, Vermont's sister looked a shade browner than she had done on the doorstep. "What a way you lose whole heap of weight," the Old Lady commented.

"And you gain 'nuff, like Gina..." Imelda said, shocked to see Queenie overweight, grey-haired, and looking ten years older than her age.

"How is Gina?" the Old Lady asked.

Imelda looked up, a pained, tormented expression on her face.

"Yuh never hear?"

"Hear what?"

"Gina dead. Same thing what take Poppa."

"I was only yuh brother wife. Why should any one tell me 'bout Gina?"

The Old Lady felt bitter that her husband's younger sister, the sibling she was closest too, had passed away and nobody thought to at least let her know. Now she had to take the grief too late. She got up hastily to make some tea, taking care to make her displeasure obvious.

"She passed quickly, she never suffer," Imelda called after, offering some small token of good news.

"No, but I did."

Imelda's eyes were like the grey which was swallowing the brown of her hair. She gazed into the fire, then down at her thin shaking hands.

"I know you blame us for Monty going," she began, "but we couldn't do anything to change his mind."

Imelda chose her words carefully. "We know he loved you. To this day, Vermont love you."

The Old Lady sucked viciously through her teeth. "Love isn't going to buy me bread to feed the pickney."

Imelda followed the Old Lady into the kitchen. She didn't know how much of this was hurting Queenie for, as ever, her sister-in-law was putting up a stoic front. Imelda stood by the old wooden table.

"Clifton grow up now?" she asked an obvious question. The Old Lady caught her forearm on the side of the boiling pot and winced loudly.

"Yuh a'right?"

"Just a lickle burn," she replied, examining the injury. She rubbed it quickly, using some ointment from out of one of the wall cupboards. Then continuing she said, "Zukie grow up now too."

"Zukie?"

"Your brother second son. Him leave me pregnant with him. I never get to tell him." She took a bag of flour from a cupboard on the wall and, with a sprinkle of water, began to knead a few cupfuls. "See him deh," she said, pointing to the living room wall opposite, through the open kitchen door.

Imelda followed the finger, open-mouthed, and stood before the school portrait of Zukie on the wall. She studied the photograph for a moment, physically moved by how much the boy looked like her brother.

"You coulda tell one ah we," she called back to Queenie.

"Unuh turn invisible. There wasn't a Michaels around. Like the magician assistant, unuh all disappear wid him." The Old Lady beat the flour with vigorous zeal.

"Why yuh so bitter? Can't you forgive? Everybody make mistakes."

The Old Lady slammed her fist into the dough, scattering flour all over the work top. She turned to face Imelda. There was flour on Queenie's spectacles, but rage towered inside her. When she spoke her voice was surprisingly calm.

"Yes, Imelda I am bitter. Me cyaan forget nor forgive. Monty never even look back. Didn't even look back 'pon the boy I have to him, never mind the one inna me belly. None of your side even acknowledge dem. None ah unuh. You all stuck together when push come to shove, yuh all put the blame on me. Me never have to pray to God for him to born and look like Monty. I did hate my belly and like God curse me, that boy born and look exactly like you people."

Rising unsteadily out of her seat, Imelda began to beat her bosom with conviction. "Oh God! God, Queenie, I swear none of we knew about the baby." Imelda's voice was quaking with hurt. She started to weep steadily. "How could we know? How could we be so wicked as to know you was carrying another chile and not tell our brother?"

"You tell me."

"Our own flesh and blood. You never told Monty. You coulda tell him yuhself."

"What was I suppose to do, eh? Go to Piccadilly train station and announce it over the speaker? Advertise 'pon radio? How many times I have to tell you, Vermont wasn't there."

Imelda sank slowly back into her creaky seat and

dabbed at her cheeks with a white handkerchief. "I still think you coulda mek the effort to find him," she remarked solemnly. If Queenie had made just a little effort, she would have discovered that her ex-husband didn't live a million miles from where she lived.

Minutes passed in silence. Outside, the rain began to fall heavily.

"Why can't we be friends?" Imelda vainly implored.

"Because we never have been. What is the purpose of this visit after all these years? You want to be their Aunty all of a sudden? Yuh t'ink Clifton gwine remember you, yuh t'ink Zukie gwine care?"

The Old Lady removed her spectacles, wiped them clean with her apron, then placed them back on her face which was gleaming with perspiration. "I know you too well Imelda, an' I know you come here for somet'ing." She fixed Imelda a steady glare. "What is it?"

Imelda lowered her eyes to the simmering pot. " Monty, Vermont wants to see his boy."

There was a pause before the Old Lady erupted.

"I don't want to listen to any of this," she shouted, struggling to maintain her composure. She threw her hands up in the air, flicking flour everywhere. There was no way she was going to let the boys' father come strolling into their lives now that they were big and grown up, after she had done all the hard work of raising them. Imelda pleaded with her for several minutes, but the Old Lady was adamant. It was non-negotiable.

"They'll see him!" Imelda assured her tearfully. "You cyan stop them. Them old enough. Yuh so cantankerous and stubborn. If it wasn't for that, Monty woulda come

55

back long time! He loved that boy. He woulda do anyt'ing fe you. All you had to do was click your fingers. How could you keep that pregnancy from him? How could you? If he had known you were pregnant, he would never have gone away. All he ever talked about was you and his boy."

Queenie made a strong effort to blank out all her sister-in-law's words, but she was unable to. Imelda made one final plea. Quietly, her voice just above a whisper, she said, "Please Queenie, he needs to see his boy. Don't deny a dying man his last wish."

ROUGH-CUT, ONE of the Grange crew, crossed bow-legged over Claremont Road, the busiest stretch of the Moss Side frontline, heading towards the new Caribbean takeaway. The smell of fried food met his nostrils. It was lunchtime and Rough was hungry. Very hungry. He could eat an elephant. He pulled the purple Kangol down over his eyes and stepped quickly into the shop.

It was one of three outlets in the area offering 'back-ah-yard' style food and had only been open a short while, yet it had already become a meeting point for various local hustlers who paused long enough in their work to have a snack. As far as Rough knew, the restaurant was not being taxed yet, and he had been sent down to check it out for the Grange and start talking percentages.

Clearly the restaurant was doing good business, Rough thought, as he scanned the menu on the wall above him for his order, making a mental note to come back in the morning to try the restaurant's 'world famous' organic porridge, in peanut, banana or corn meal. There were quite a few customers for that time of day, and he had heard that the place was usually rammed come evening time. The kitchen had already earned the reputation, in places even further than Manchester, that it was the place to check out for anybody who wanted some genuine, undiluted Yard cooking. Judging by the aroma which wafted like a sunny breeze out from the kitchen, Rough knew that he was in for a good treat.

His order taken, Rough turned his gaze to the restaurant manager. A man in his thirties, whose shiny black face still possessed the polish of years in the Caribbean sun, and whose permanently watery eyes were a reminder that he thought often of his homeland. From the portable stereo on the shelf behind him, a Yard tape was blasting out versions of dancehall rhythms from a live session. Stone Love were on the wire and firing.

"So what happen?" Rough asked the man eventually, fixing him with a business-like stare.

The manager, an unsmiling, full-bearded man, who had 'seen it all before', merely nodded at the youth in the Kangol. He had a serious expression on his face, as if he was expecting trouble at any moment. He looked as if he was prepared for it. Maybe he had a baseball bat behind the counter, Rough wondered. He suddenly didn't feel so confident anymore. Maybe he should wait for back-up. It wasn't easy at the best of times to convince a proprietor to part with a portion of his week's takings for the sake of good community relations. Often it was those proprietors who had come straight from Yard, that were the toughest nuts to crack. They were stubborn and adamant that they would die resisting if it came to that. Rough hoped it wouldn't come to that. He studied the frozen expression on the man's face once more. He could read it clearly now. It was threatening: I know who you are, but you don't know who I am. So don't test, the man's eyes told him.

Finally one of the other assistants came out of the kitchen with Rough's order. Beef stew and rice. It was his favourite and his mouth watered as the aroma drifted up to him through the tin-foil container.

"Alright...," he said pulling out a couple of notes, "get me an Irish as well..."

The assistant ducked into the over-size fridge and pulled out a bottle of Irish Moss. Rough handed over the money and waited for his change. Laden with his supplies, he turned to make his way out the door. In that moment the winter sun flashed briefly through the glass door and splashed on the manager's forehead. The bead of sweat trickling down the manager's face caught Rough's eye. Maybe, he considered, it was because the heat from the kitchen was warming up the restaurant, but then again, maybe it wasn't. It helped his confidence to assume the latter.

"So," he asked casually, turning back to the manager, "who owns this place then?"

"You mean who control it?" the man asked with a defiant smirk on his face.

Rough nodded.

"You're too late," the manager said, jerking his head

58

towards the street door from where a sharp, cold breeze had just blown in. "Ah dem run t'ings."

Rough turned, slowly. Teeko and a big belly, giant of a youth named Slim, were standing behind him. Their expressions were stone cold and Teeko, his hands dancing hypnotically before him, had taken up a horse stance.

Rough Cut made his move quick, hurling himself at the Piper Mill soldiers. Somehow, he managed to bulldoze his way past them and through the front door, but his bow-legs only made it as far as the kerb. Teeko launched himself airborne with a flying tackle and wrestled Rough to the ground. Slim was right behind him and clubbed the Grange boy unconscious with what felt like a heavy, blunt instrument.

It was Rough's bad luck that he chose to be at the takeaway at the wrong time. Teeko and Slim bundled Rough into the boot of a BMW and sped off. In the takeaway, the customers eagerly discussed what they had witnessed, each person giving their side of the story of what really went down, but the manager went about his business, seeing no evil nor hearing no evil.

HIS GREY-GREEN eyes wandered around the unfamiliar room. One of the walls was covered by two large, Victorian oak bookcases, filled with books. In a large fireplace, the embers of a real fire glowing dimly, refusing to surrender, cast a warm light over the darkened room. A Victorian walnut roll-top bureau

59

rested in a quiet subdued corner of the room. An ornate wall lamp burned above it.

Zukie felt uncomfortable and apprehensive. He had spent the whole day with Paradise at her father's house, talking about the old days and it was now early evening. He was still slightly tense about the situation. He kept expecting Pastor Browne to step in at any moment. A spliff would ease his nerves, but he didn't have the bottle to build one. His head buzzed, building up momentum for something, he didn't know what.

Nervously, he took a few steps towards the nineteenth century mahogany desk. On it were framed pictures of Preach's wife, Mona Browne, the boys, Manessah and Euphrates in black graduation caps and gowns, and of their daughter, Paradise. Zukie touched the hand painted cigar box on the desk, hardly believing he was in the home of Mr Big Shot, Pastor Roy Browne, a prominent figure in Manchester's black community. Sighing, he made himself comfortable on one of the three seater settees and slipped deep into the soft leather.

Paradise Browne was standing in front of him now, flashing a cherry-red smile. He noticed the blazing heat from the fire. She had revived the dying embers. On the coffee table she'd placed a bottle of Chardonnay and two crystal wine glasses. Still smiling, she eased herself gracefully down onto the sofa next to him. Every muscle in Zukie's body tensed.

Leaning forward towards the mahogany coffee table, she opened the bottle with a quick twist and delicately poured wine into one of the glasses.

"Want a drink?" she asked smiling, the bottle poised

60

over his glass.

"Well," he swallowed, "you know, I don't really, you know... drink."

"Don't drink?! Why not? Don't be a prude!" She spilled some wine into his glass. "Come on, it will loosen you up."

He didn't want to be loosened up, he wanted to stay together. He took a cautious sip from his filled glass, relaxing only slightly.

"That's better," she enthused. "Want to watch a video?"

"Your dad's church sermons? No thanks."

She laughed. "No, you won't find any preaching here." She got up and slotted a video into the machine. Two naked forms filled the screen.

Zukie blinked, his face flushing. Swallowing the rest of his wine in one gulp, he started to rise and said quickly, "I've been here too long. I'd better go."

"No!" she shouted, a desperate look in her dark eyes. Then quietly. "Please stay. Zukie, I'm lonely."

He nodded and sat back down on the sofa.

"Want a smoke?" she asked, flicking the video off.

"Smoke what?"

"Anything, coke, black, sensi."

"I man don't smoke chemicals."

"It's only a joke. Relax, Zukie."

Zukie stayed silent, watching her body as she fleeted off the sofa and rummaged through the drawer of her father's bureau. This wasn't what he was expecting from her. He wasn't sure if he liked the way she was behaving, but at the same time he felt comfortable with her.

"Well, I'm going to have a smoke," she said. Her voice was husky, a little nervous. She came and sat down next to him again, closer this time. As he watched her skillfully shaping the Rizla into a five sheeter, she started to hum a deep melody, forming the words of a song. Her voice trembled with emotion.

When, when I die,
I want the Lord
To carry me high...

She paused only to light up.

And if, if I should fall,
His strong arms will
Carry me home...

Eyes firmly closed, face intense, smoke drifting from her open mouth, she passed the spliff to Zukie.

Her voice was mellow and soothing. Smoke billowed through Zukie's nostrils. The spliff was beautiful, prime sensimilla. The very best weed.

"I like the way you caress those notes, Paradise," he said staring entranced at her. "You got good vocals."

She fidgeted with the hem of her white cotton dress.

"Daddy says my voice is like Mummy's before they got married." Then she began to titter, fixing her eyes on him. "I can still see your Mum dragging you and your brother to our church."

Zukie inhaled deeply, trying to erase the image. His headache was abating slightly. "I remember how you used to heal people," he said. "You still healin' people and all that?"

"Yeah," she smiled ardently at him, her eyes roving over his body. "I guess they kind of heal themselves. Most of it's all in their heads."

"You mean most of it's all a big con." He blew smoke out.

"No," she said defensively. "I have a gift. I really do cure them. When the spirit takes you anything is possible."

Smoke drifted between them. Now he felt relaxed, but still confused. Was this really the little church girl he used to know? As Paradise got up to get more drink, Zukie's thoughts began to wander. He thought about his brother, Clifton, and how differently things had turned out for them. How whatever Cliff did the Old Lady still loved him. She was willing to believe anything he told her. All that crap about being a sales rep. Cliff was living a huge lie, just running and running and trying to run away from himself. But the Old Lady couldn't see it. Meanwhile, she was always quick to jump on Zukie's arse. She didn't seem to care that he was trying to live righteous, the way they had been brought up. All she could see was that Cliff was bringing home corn and, in her eyes, that meant her elder son was doing well while he, the younger son, was unemployed and that made him an outcast.

But why was he thinking about all this? It was definitely the wrong place and the wrong time. Right now he didn't want to think about Cliff, or the Old Lady, or the shit that was going down on the streets. The buzz the last two days was about the gun t'ing, but that had nothing to do with him. Not right now anyway.

All he wanted to think about was Paradise. He wanted her.

CLIFTON WAS LYING on the sofa in the Old Lady's living room flicking between the stations on the television, when the call came through on his mobile.

"Storm, dem have Rough."

It was Lewty, calling mobile to mobile. A moment's silence passed between them as Storm contemplated.

"Who, Beast?"

"No. A coupla G's. Sounds like Piper Mill."

He told Storm as much as he knew. That Rough was in the takeaway when a couple of Johnny-too-bads jumped him and put him in the boot of their car.

"Shit!" Storm kissed his teeth. That was bad news, that was really bad news. But he was expecting something like this.

"So what d'you want me to do?" Lewty asked anxiously.

"But you don't know for sure it was the Pipers?"

Lewty sniffed on the other end of the phone. Why were they going over the same ground? He hoped that if it was he who had been attacked, Storm wouldn't waste time asking questions, but steam into whoever it was with guns blazing.

"We gotta do something, chief," he stressed.

Storm's head was pounding. It bothered him that he hadn't been able to make it out to the hospital to see his daughter, but events were unfolding at such a rapid rate. There had been several calls to deal with throughout the day. Problems of one type or another to sort out. And now this. It worried him, worried him a lot that instead of being able to wind down his side of the operations, he was getting more involved.

"Okay," he decided finally, "first, get confirmation that it's definitely Pipers. Then call me."

"Is that it?" Lewty asked with a tone of incredulity in his voice.

"Yeah, for now. That's it. Tell everybody to stay calm and stay alive."

Lewty grunted his acknowledgement and the line went dead.

"ZUKIE?"

He didn't recognise Paradise's voice instantly. He was exhausted and his body felt like lead.

"You okay? Zukie wake up."

"Wha'?"

He forced his eyes open, dimly making out her outline. Her face was pushing towards his, smelling of strong alcohol. On the coffee table were three empty bottles and the remains of as many spliffs in the ashtray. She sat down beside him and began to massage his stomach gently. He felt the heat, his muscles relaxed and his penis hardened. He moaned as she reached down and stroked him teasingly.

"I guess," she said smiling, "you'll have to stay the rest of the night. You have no choice."

Without warning she pulled her cotton dress slowly and seductively over her head. Zukie gulped seeing her dark bosom within the lacy white bra, her slender waist, the black panties.

"Well, are you going to make me stand like this all night?" she asked with a seductive smile.

Slowly, cautiously, Zukie caressed her breasts. The moment he touched the bra he felt a surge in his crotch.

"You don't mind, do you?" he asked, slightly apprehensive.

She laughed.

"Zukie, I thought you would be an expert at this."

She caressed his neck softly with both her hands, then pulled him towards her and kissed him, long and deep. Her tongue darting in and out of his mouth. Zukie closed his eyes and felt her soft, moist lips on his. He was quivering at the thighs, unwilling to resist. He felt his chest rising and falling, as he thought the most pleasant thoughts. He stroked her arched, naked, brown-skinned back and let his hand slip under her panties to her pert, round bottom. He breathed more heavily. He fumbled in his pocket for the condom he always carried, just in case. She led him by the hand up the stairs, to her bedroom. Before long they were between the sheets. Just as he was about to enter her she suddenly tensed.

"It's my first time," she confessed. She wanted it to be special and she wanted it to be with Zukie. She had always fancied Zukie and now he was here it was like a dream. She had waited a long time for this moment.

"Don't worry," Zukie tried to assure her, "I'll go easy."

She closed her eyes tight as he eased himself inside her, felt his chest on top of her, his hot breath in her ear, breathing fast, faster. And as he pushed himself deeper and deeper inside her, she held on to his tight bottom, as if her life depended on it.

Zukie was not in control of his pelvis, nor of his cock, which threatened to explode at any minute. Paradise felt too good to be true. He loved the way she looked, her wide and sensual mouth, her breasts. He loved the way she moved and he particularly liked the way she held him close. As he tried to maintain a steady rhythm on top, he flattered her with compliments and showered her with kisses all over her beautiful body.

"Rock with me," he said to her. "Does it feel good for you too?"

Paradise nodded her head quickly, her eyes still shut tight.

IT WAS A relatively short journey, but for Rough Cut in the boot of the car, it seemed to go on forever. He feared for his life, for not only was he outnumbered, they were sure to be armed. He wished he had his lucky hat with him, but the Kangol had fallen off outside the restaurant. He felt vulnerable without it. When the car pulled to a stop he began to panic and out of terror more than anything else, kicked his legs furiously against the door of the boot, as he heard the lock click from the outside.

Teeko and Slim managed to jump back just in time

before the boot door flew up towards them. At almost the same instant, Rough flew out of the boot looking dazed and bloodied. The Piper men were still rooted to the ground as Rough, a vengeful look on his face, threw himself at them, knocking them down. Rough didn't stop to pause, but ran across the wasteground as fast as his legs could carry him, in the only direction that seemed to make sense — straight ahead, with the two men not far behind him. Suddenly a tall wall loomed up ahead. Rough threw his head back quickly and saw the Piper men right behind him. He turned again and accelerated towards the wall.

Ordinarily, he might have made it, but Rough didn't have a moment to assess the height accurately, nor time to adjust his stride before he hurled himself high into the air, with his arms reaching upwards as high as they could go. He missed the top of the wall and tumbled back down at the feet of his pursuers. His shoulder hit the ground first, then his head, then the rest of him. He crashed down on the ground with a thud.

He only had a moment to consider his wrenched shoulder and his back pounding with pain for, at the same time, his pursuers unleashed a series of kicks to his head and face and back and chest. He only just made it to his feet, his back against the brick wall. He protected himself as best as he could with his hands, but there were too many blows and they came with such ferocity. Something was not quite right. He tried to lift his legs, but couldn't. Then he saw something shining on one of his assailants hands. It looked like he was wearing rings on his fingers, but Rough was afraid it wasn't. He felt a nick across his cheek and his face was cut. The next blow would leave an inch-long horizontal scar across the bridge of his nose. Rough felt blood trickling down to his lips, tasted its slightly salty taste in his mouth. His assailant lashed out several more times until Rough stumbled forwards and fell to the ground.

Teeko and Slim continued kicking him until they were both exhausted, cursing the Grange boy. But they didn't want to kill him. They wanted him to survive as a warning to the Grange leader.

With his face slashed and knife wounds in his chest, Rough managed to crawl out of the wasteground on to the road in front, after the Pipers disappeared. It seemed like he had laid there for hours, when a young boy on a mountain bike found him.

Seeing her son in intensive care fighting for his life had put grey hairs on Rough Cut's mother's head. The doctors said he had a fifty-fifty chance of making it through, but the woman kept the faith, the Lord would see her son through.

TRIBUTES STARTED POURING in to the pirate radio stations in honour of Fluxy. D.J. Bagga Worries, a much respected 'cultural' disc jockey, dedicated an entire hour to the tributes on his *Late Night Jam* programme on Frontline Radio. He himself had known Fluxy personally, and played strictly Bob Marley tunes for the rest of the evening in honour of his friend:

"Good evening, who's calling the Late Night Jam?"

"Yeah, this is Trigga, calling from Moss Side... Bagga Don, I waan yuh play a record for me idren Fluxy, who pass away the other day... And fe him family, his lickle breddah Marvin an' Mrs Ellis..."

"Yeah, respect fe dat selection," Bagga agreed. "So tell me somet'ing, you an' Fluxy were idren?"

"Yeah man, me an' him grow up together, eat outta one dutch pot together, play football an' all cricket together..."

"So tell me somet'ing, what do you think about all the gun violence in Manchester right now?"

"Well really an' truly," the caller answered earnestly, "when a innocent man like Fluxy can just get 'baddap!' when he's just goin' about his business not troublin' anyone, it's dread."

"So what would your advice be to all the gun men listening in to the Late Night Jam?"

"I would just say put up the gun, every an' anyone ah unuh, seen."

"Words of wisdom my brother man... This tune is going out to the late great Glenn Ellis...many of you know him as Fluxy, and to the Ellis family, that's Marvin and Mrs Ellis. And that's coming from Trigga out there in the Moss Side area. To the Ellis family, your friends are thinking about you, here's the sounds of the reggae king Bob Marley..."

The airwaves filled with No Woman No Cry, the words even more poignant. Everybody who heard it felt for the mother who had lost her son in such tragic circumstances, the mother who was now thinking about when she used to sit, with her son, in a government yard in Moss Side, observing the hypocrites who mingled with the good people...

70

Bagga followed up the selection with a version by Beenie Man, the lyrics of which still echoed on the airwaves several hours later:

No momma, nuh cry — every day another ghetto yout' die
No momma nuh cry

"And who's calling the Late Night Jam?"
"This is Pauline, from Cheetham Hill. Play a dedication for Fluxy for me... I miss him bad."

TWO POWERFUL ARMS were yanking his dreadlocks violently. He remembered he wasn't at home asleep, but in Paradise's bedroom. The morning light was streaming in through the window. They'd made love and he'd fallen asleep. For a moment his eyes focused on the room. The pine wardrobe, the cuddly toys, the small portable colour TV, the pine bed where they'd been lost in each other for hours.

Zukie's feet felt like feathers and his head like lead. Manessah and Euphrates, both built like body builders, were knocking him about like a rag doll.

"What the hell are you doing in my house? In my daughter's bed?!" a voice was screaming. Zukie saw that the angry voice belonged to Pastor Browne.

"Hold him good," the Pastor ordered. He slapped Zukie across the face repeatedly until his cheeks burned like fire. Paradise tried in vain to save him from her father's wrath. Her pleas were futile, and the Pastor turned his anger on her with blows to her head and body.

"Daddy!" she screamed, "Daddy! Please Daddy, stop!"

Mona Browne leaped forward to rescue her daughter and, at the same time, shouted at Zukie to get his clothes and leave.

The last thing Zukie heard as he fled the room was Pastor Browne roaring like a madman:

"I'll get you for this! I know who you are!! I'll find you, you rasta fucker!! Then I'll kill you!! Yuh hear me? I'm going to kill you!! Fucccccccccckkkkkkkkaaaaaaah!!"

THE FRONT DOOR closed with a gentle click. Footsteps shuffled along the protective plastic covering the hall carpet. A soft tinkle of keys, the whir and click of a bicycle chain as it glided through the mechanism. A loud cough repeated twice.

Clifton stirred awake with a dull, nagging ache in his stomach and a harsh buzzing sound in his ears. For a few brief seconds he was incapable of recalling his surroundings. He'd fallen asleep on the settee in the living room. It was Sunday morning. His mind was in a turmoil. Sudden, vivid images flooded into his head.

The rain was still falling heavily outside, making a noise like hailstones. He had been asleep hours but, once again, it was a troubled sleep from which he awoke several times.

The living room door opened and Zukie entered. He tip-toed slowly across the room aware of his brother's presence. Clifton coughed. Zukie looked down at his brother. Clifton sat back placing his feet upon the scuffed surface of the pine coffee table. It was an uncomfortable moment. Neither knew what to say to the other. Hatred for his brother reflected in Zukie's eyes. He hated everything about him. He hated the way Cliff talked, the way he walked, the clothes he wore. He even hated his brother's close-cropped hair and the parting in it. Bust most of all, he hated Cliff for who he was. They simply froze as they stared at each other. Then Clifton shifted uneasily in his chair. He blinked then looked again at his younger brother. He remembered Zukie as being a bit shy and a bit of a wimp, but essentially a nice guy and warmhearted, who looked up to his elder brother. It seemed strange to see him staring in this way with so much hate.

Looking at them, a total stranger would have found it hard to believe they were brothers. Zukie's skin colour was too pale and Clifton's too dark for them to be alike. But they were one blood, same mother same father.

"So what happen, yout'?" Clifton said eventually, trying to diffuse the situation. He didn't want a bust-up just now.

Zukie simply kissed his teeth.

"What the fuck was that for?" Clifton asked, now pissed off.

"What are you doing back here?"

"I live here, don't I?" Clifton's jaw tightened and the cleft in his chin became more pronounced.

"Do you?" Zukie asked unimpressed. "I thought you was a big high roller now with a place of your own. Why d'you have to come back here?"

"Well at least the Old Lady's happy to see me..."

"Yeah sure, she's happy to see her son, Clifton. She in't happy to see no bad bwai called Storm."

"So that's what all this is about?" Clifton asked. "Why don't you just res' yuhself, man. And where the hell have you been anyway? You stay out all night and don't even let her know where you are."

Zukie didn't even want to hear it. Any respect he previously held for his elder brother had long since disappeared, and he felt that Clifton was the last one he would take lectures from. Besides he'd had a rough morning.

"It's none of your business where I've been!" he spat, with a shake of his sandy-coloured dreadlocks. "Your business is cocaine in't it? Yeah there's a lot of money in that white powder in't there? When you wind up in jail doing twenty years you'll have enough time to count all that money, in pennies!"

"You sound like yuh just jealous," Clifton said, with a serious look on his face.

"Don't make me laugh. All you're dealin' with is vanities. I couldn't be jealous of that. And up to now, how much man have you killed, Storm? You think the Old Lady's going to be happy when she finds out? I could never be jealous of that."

For the first time Cliff seemed to be nervous. He watched his brother's eyes closely. He wouldn't, would he?

"Don't even think about it, Zukie," he warned. "The Old Lady's got enough worries to deal with."

Zukie simply smiled sardonically. However much respect Storm earned out on the street, when he came to his mother's house, he was simply Clifton Michaels.

Despite their ages, the Old Lady still had an almost magical hold over them. Neither of them would dream of giving the Old Lady anything less than the maximum respect due to the woman who had given birth and raised them. The woman who had disciplined them strictly throughout their childhood .

"So," Zukie asked sarcastically, "how much man have you killed now, don man?"

"What are you talking about, I've never killed anyone," Storm answered perplexed.

Zukie laughed, a short, cold laugh. "That's not what I hear. A Piper Mill man got blasted. Everyone says you did it."

"Look, I've never killed anyone!" Clifton insisted again. He understood why suspicion was on him and the Grange. Sure, the Grange were having run-ins with Piper Mill, but that didn't mean he wanted him dead. Fluxy had 'nuff enemies. Even if he had planned on getting rid of him, Storm would have had to join the back of the queue. Anybody could have killed the Piper Mill leader.

Zukie looked at his brother unimpressed.

"But you see what I mean don't you, every time you come home, you bring some whole heap of problems with you, like everything you touch turns to dust. You use this place like a hotel, whenever you want to lie low, and that's slack. What's the matter man, you in't got no shame? 'Cause personally, I'm full of shame for you, man. Out on the streets when people are talking about 'bwoy, the Grange posse do this and the Grange posse do that', I'm just happy they don't know we're related."

"What the hell do *you* know?" Clifton asked quietly.

"*You* don't have to believe me. But if you put any ideas into the Old Lady's head, I'll..." Clifton turned away from Zukie and walked towards the sink, searching for the right words. "...Look, we don't have to be like this," he continued, his voice still low. "We're one blood. We shouldn't be fighting each other. You don't like the way I'm livin', well that's cool. But I'm still your brother. You can't do nothing about that. I got your back covered, bro. When all this is over I'll hook you up good. You wanna do your music, you'll have the backing. Believe, man."

Zukie smiled, obviously amused.

"You got every last detail planned, innit Cliff?" He leaned against the wall. "What you going to do when it go wrong?"

"When what goes wrong?"

"You're the clever one, Cliff, you tell me."

A silence fell between them.

A DAZZLING WINTER sun filtered through the stained glass windows, glorifying the magnificence of the new, modern Church of Zion situated on Great Western Street in Rusholme..

Its seats were pure mahogany, its aisles carpeted in a luxurious, deep green pile. At each window were heavy, ochre-coloured velvet curtains. It was a warm, comfortable church its minister could be proud of, and Pastor Browne was fiercely proud.

Standing before his congregation Pastor Browne

closed his eyes, opened trembling lips, and began his lesson. Paradise, head of the choir and normally found seated behind and to the left of her father, was noticeably absent.

"Let us go to perfection..." Pastor Browne continued, his usually composed, round face bursting with sweat.

"Praise God!" cried a voice.

"Hallelujah!" the congregation responded, latching on to the Spirit within the church, within themselves.

"Perfection, brothers and sisters, laying down the foundation of repentance."

"Save your souls!" someone called out.

"Praise God and live!" someone else bawled out feverishly.

"Repentance...." Browne began again, picking up the Spirit, ".... of dead, *dead* works and of faith towards God." His right fist ploughed into the pulpit with a crash. "Let us speak of baptism and of the laying of hands, and of the resurrection of the dead, and of eternal Judgement...."

"Day of Judgement!" someone intoned.

"Praise the Lord!" another person commanded.

"These are the last days!" cried a large woman in the front as Pastor Browne went on:

"Children having children, pestilence, earthquakes and famine."

"Christ our Lord cometh. Prepare. Prepare!" came another cry.

Pastor Browne looked down at the tiled ground surrounding the pulpit. The sky outside suddenly darkened, and wind rattled against the windows. Reaching down into his clerical gown, the Pastor took a pair of black framed reading glasses from a case and placed them on his face. He flicked the pages of the Holy Bible before him and began again, silently, not sure where his unplanned sermon was leading.

"Turning now to the Scriptures, to brother Isiah, the Prophet." The words stuck in his throat.

The church was silent. Waiting. No coughs, no murmurs. Slowly his head began to bow down towards the pages of Isiah, the words becoming more and more misty. Despair saw its chance and seized the moment. He kneaded the sides of his pulpit with his hands, a tear spilling from the small pools on the insides of his glass lenses. Soon the whole page of Isiah was damp.

In his head he saw the light-skinned boy, long knotted hair on top of his Paradise's naked brown flesh, sweat glistening on his body. Two bodies entwined, locked in pleasure, oblivious to everything but their lovemaking. The boy was concentrating hard, lifting his body gently up to admire the girl's breasts, jerking with each thrust. And with each jerk she moaned, bawling and laughing simultaneously. He was fucking her mercilessly, furiously and she was enjoying it. His step-daughter, Paradise, who he had nurtured from a young age to be pure, so that he himself may take that first, tasteful bite of her ripening fruit, had been defiled by a dirty rastaman. It pained him so much, his heart pounded in double time and his eyes filled with an expression of seething rage.

A loud murmur of concern brought him back to the church and his congregation. He'd been silent for some time. Wiping tears from his glasses with a clean handkerchief, he carefully placed them back in their

79

case. In a trembling low voice, words floated out of his mouth.

He cleared his throat. Rubbing it, he was conscious of a burning sensation in his chest. Nevertheless he struggled on with his dwindling sermon. "Let us consider the things written and seen by the prophet Elijah... Sorry, the prophet Isiah."

He closed his eyes, trying to blank out the faces before him. "You all may have noticed that my daughter, Paradise, cannot be with us today to sing with the choir. Unfortunately, she has met with a bad accident, and I hope you will all remember her in your prayers. Pray that she will be able to join us next week. Please, let us all rise."

Again the Pastor's heart raced away as his thoughts drifted back to his daughter's 'infidelity', because that's how he saw it, she was unfaithful to *him*. After all he had done for her. After he had done everything possible to ensure that she lived a comfortable life, this is how she rewarded him, sleeping with a dirty, low class rastafarian in *his* house! He felt hot. How could she have done this?

Suddenly Pastor Browne fell, the pulpit crashing down on him. His heart tightened and he tried to catch his breath. His mouth was dry and bitter. Darkness threatened to overcome him. Somewhere in the darkness he heard his wife's voice calling his name.

INFECTIOUS, MILDLY HYSTERICAL laughter

bounced off the walls, the harmonies of a quartet of 'sisters', 'female cousins', 'aunts' or simply 'women-folk', fanning themselves and busy gossiping together on a Sunday afternoon, in the Old Lady's living room with the heating turned up too high.

Seated in the room were four of the sisters from church, sipping steaming hot tea from the Old Lady's best china set, the one she only brought out on special occasions. Leaning against one another, they laughed, like schoolgirls in a convent, sharing the intimacy of the latest gossip.

It was late afternoon and church had been abandoned hours before.

The aroma of seasoned roast chicken filled the living room, along with the tantalising smell of traditional Caribbean rice and peas.

"You nevah tell me seh you get new furniture. Is when yuh get it?" Sister Anthony asked the Old Lady. Tall and dark, she was Chico's mother.

The Old Lady looked around at the brand new black leather three piece suite, the Axminster carpets and the burgundy velvet curtains that now adorned her house. She didn't know how to answer having only just discovered it all herself. The new furniture was waiting on her return from church. All the old furniture had been thrown out. She could only assume that it was a surprise present from Clifton. He was always promising to replace her old stuff and he liked to surprise her with gifts whenever he stayed at home.

"Perhaps she have a secret man and nuh tell we," Sister Anthony teased.

"What?" the Jamaican Indian, Sister Knowles asked,

cocking a deaf ear towards Sister Anthony. "A secret *pan*?"

"Is only me son, Clifton. Him look after me good as you know."

"Bwai, him must be a millionaire," Sister Jones stated, looking around at the good quality furniture suspiciously.

"If him was a millionaire yuh t'ink she would be here talking to we?" Sister Anthony asked breaking into laughter. "She woulda be cock up inna one hammock 'pon Negril beach."

"Still," the diminutive Sister Jones said feebly, "he's a good boy and he's doing well." She wished she could say the same for her boy, Felix, or Hair Oil as he was known to his friends. He didn't seem to be doing anything with his life.

The Old Lady smiled proudly. "Pastor Browne help him when he was a young boy," she said. "Wid him studying."

"Poor Pastor Browne!" Sister Jones declared solemnly, her mind drifting back to the sensational events of that morning in church.

Sister Anthony spluttered on her tea. "Poor Pastor Browne?" Roaring with husky laughter. "Nothing don't seriously wrong wid him. The only part of him what hurt is him pride. He'll get over it."

"What?" Sister Knowles asked, wriggling herself forward.

"She said...." Sister Palmer began to say to the hearing-impaired woman, then changed her mind quickly. "Oh never mind."

"He'll be all right," Sister Anthony continued, "faster

than he can preach righteousness."

Laughter erupted in the room. Sister Knowles laughed because everyone else in the room was laughing. Only Sister Jones sat nervously, staring silently into her cup of tea. She failed to see what was so funny about their spiritual leader collapsing? She fixed her gaze steadily on Sister Anthony. "Dotty, we shouldn't mock the afflicted."

"Is who mocking the afflicted?" Sister Anthony asked, a smile teasing the corners of her lips, her black eyes glinting wickedly.

"What? What she say?" Sister Knowles asked, scanning the circle of faces.

"So when yuh ah go buy a hearing aid, you fool!" Sister Anthony yelled.

Sister Knowles laughed.

"What do I want lemonade for? I still drinking me tea," she said.

Sister Jones sank her small frame into the comfort of the new settee. She continued from where she left off.

"It isn't christian, that's all," she muttered, "we should be offering our concern for the Pastor's health in prayer."

Sister Anthony studied the other women's faces before speaking. "Amelia, darling gyal, *you* can go pray fe him, but me saving me prayers for the *really* afflicted. People like meself, who never know the use of a good man from me lef' Jamaica an' come ah England!"

Sister Jones and Sister Anthony were close friends much like their sons Hair Oil and Chico. But on this point, they would agree to differ before they came to blows. Sister Anthony couldn't understand why her friend was always trying to deify the Pastor when they all knew that he was an ordinary man like any other man, with the same faults, and his only exceptional talent was that he could chat well enough to keep a congregation of 200 churchgoers transfixed every Sunday. He certainly wasn't, like Sister Jones would have it, one of the Twelve Disciples.

"Well," the Old Lady interceded, clearing her throat, "I wasn't aware of him being sick before."

Sister Anthony's mouth fired into action. "Yes, but I hear that him daughter, Miss Paradise, mek him know his heart was weak."

Peals of laughter unfolded. They were all acquainted with the hottest gossip in the church, of how Pastor Browne came home to find his cherubic daughter romping with abandon in bed with an intruder. Nobody knew who the man was. They only knew that Pastor Browne wanted to keep the whole thing as quiet as possible.

"I'll go and make some more tea." The Old Lady excused herself quickly, leaving them chatting and laughing.

"Clifton really was sweet-looking when he was a young baby boy!" Sister Knowles called after her, admiring a photograph on the wall.

The Old Lady smiled, still drunk with pride at her elder son who had furnished her home so immaculately.

She hadn't been in the kitchen long before a deafening, electronic pounding blasted from above. The bass and drums thumped and the lyrics came out crisp and clear.

"....Me have the visa buddy for the passport punny
Me want a permanent stamp fe go ah New York City
Me go a de airport me sight Kathleen
Me seh open up yuh legs IMMEDIATELY...!!!"

The Old Lady stood rooted to the spot. Her heart beating loud. Her church sisters must have heard the words also... Slackness, in her house?! And on a church day too!

Zukie hit the tape button as soon as he woke up. Shit, the lover's tape wasn't what he wanted right now. He needed some ragga to wake himself up. He hit another button and the second deck played its ragga tape. He shivered, drawing cold air into his lungs, remembering his dream. Pastor Browne was chasing him while Paradise laughed. And he was stumbling in the darkness somewhere. Heart pounding, he was cold and terrified. The Pastor had a semi-automatic and was firing. As Zukie looked down, he could see the bullets entering his body. And he thought, I'm not real. I don't exist. I'm dead. How can you kill something that's already dead?

He sniffed, his nose burned hot, the tip cold. Paradise. She was occupying his thoughts. Her curves, the soft brown skin, the suppleness, the wet, warm, succulent velvet of her entire body. He was naked between two rough, cold sheets. He sniffed repeatedly. His whole body ached. His balls were freezing, but his cock was hard like rock.

He thought the Old Lady was still in church and he had the whole house to himself, so ignoring the 'No Smoking' signs the Old Lady had plastered all over his room, Zukie lit a spliff which he'd been saving for days. He really needed a smoke. What the hell, as the Old Lady wasn't around he may as well turn up his music to boom box level. He pulled himself up to a sitting position and pulled heavily on the spliff, as he slipped into a pair of jeans. The room was throbbing with the volume from the bass boxes which crowded his room.

Suddenly the bedroom door flew open and the Old Lady stood there, hands on hips and a mean, murderous look on her face. Zukie instinctively tried to hide the spliff, but it was no use. The Old Lady had already seen it. There was nowhere to run.

"Yuh smoking ganja?! Hmmnh?! Answer me! In my house!?" The Old Lady roared.

Zukie simply looked at her and shrugged his shoulders, the fear gone in his eyes. It was only a bit of bud. What was the big deal? What could the Old Lady do anyway?

The Old Lady was almost beside herself with rage. Ordinarily, she would have slapped her son across the face and snatched the spliff from his hands, but something warned her not to. She wanted to drag him by the locks there and then, and cut off his hair which offended her so much, but she dared not. It was the look in Zukie's eyes. For the first time the Old Lady saw a look of defiance. It frightened her.

"Never think I was here did you?! This is Sunday, the day of the Lord." Perspiration gleamed on her face. "An' you up here blasting out slack music and smoking ganja! Me ah go kill yuh!"

The Old Lady didn't know what to do. Her words sounded empty, her threats had no bite. She wanted to do something. She wanted to punish him for still being in bed late on Sunday afternoon. She wanted to punish him for not being like his brother, for not being able to make her proud like he did, for not being able to buy her furniture like the furniture Clifton had bought her, which her friends were still admiring downstairs. But the power she had even the day before, seemed to have vanished and she couldn't understand why.

The loud knocking on the front door saved the stand-off. The Old Lady shot her son a reproachful glare, "What yuh standin' there for? Yuh eedyaat!! Open up the dyam door!!"

The Old Lady turned to go back downstairs, followed by her son who was still pulling on a T-shirt. She disappeared into the living room and Zukie heard her say to her church sistren, "Dyam fool pickney!"

Mona Celia Browne stood on the doorstep shaking the rain off her frilly, pink and white umbrella. Dressed in a fur coat and black high-heeled boots, she looked prim, proper and pretty rather than elegant. Unlike many of her female contemporaries she had lost little of her youthful beauty and could have passed for her daughter's older sister more easily than her mother. Her presence rooted Zukie to the spot. Holding the door open wide, his jaw dropped slightly.

"Who is it?!" The Old Lady was suddenly right next to her son, yanking the door away from him. "Mona?" Surprise filled her voice. "Mona..." She couldn't understand what Pastor Browne's wife was doing at her house nor remember when Mrs Browne last paid her a social visit. "...How nice to see you, Sister Mona! Come on in an' release yuh worries. Me nuh know why de bwai leave you outside." She squinted sideways at her son.

Sister Mona looked about nervously. "Never come fe stop too long," she said pointedly.

"Hot tea boiling. Yuh must can stop longer than five minutes."

As Mrs Browne stepped in she kept her gaze on Zukie who dropped his, as if some minuscule object on the carpet distracted him. The Old Lady noticed the uncomfortable exchange between her guest and her son and, for a moment, a thought crossed her mind. But no, it couldn't be. It just couldn't be.

"Is it about the boy?" she asked nervously.

The two women stood there in the hallway, avoiding each other's gaze. Zukie stood slightly behind, keeping quiet.

"You have visitors," Mona said solemnly, avoiding the question. Her Jamaican accent was mild.

"Just the church sisters," the Old Lady replied. "You can talk freely."

Mona's eyes became vacant and watery. "I wasn't going to come at all," she began, "but when Roy collapsed today I realised the seriousness of this... Queenie, you and I have been good friends from back home. I don't know the best way to approach this situation... Queenie, you got to help me through this, please." The two women looked directly at each other.

From the living room, a cackle of laughter burst out. The church sisters seemed to be enjoying themselves. The Old Lady's eyes flitted from Mona to Zukie and back to Mona, then back to Zukie. She saw it all in their eyes, Mona's embarrassment, Zukie's discomfort. It was him! So it was Zukie with Paradise in the Pastor's house. Her son was responsible for causing the Pastor's illness. This would cause her shame, total shame amongst her friends and church. Did her son have no respect for her? Did he have no decency? No common sense?

"I don't want to hear any of this!" She raised her voice too loud, too quickly. Suddenly everyone was in the hallway, all the church sisters, to hear what the commotion was about.

"It hurts me to tell you Mona, but yes, your son came into our house when me and my husband were away... He brought drugs and smoked them in our house... and then..." Mrs Browne breathed in deeply and sharply. She looked away, as if reluctant to finish her tale.

"Then... he took advantage of my daughter... He raped her!"

The church sisters uttered gasps of horror.

The Old Lady stared at her son's accuser stony-faced and stood up squarely to her.

"A lie! Zukie would never..."

"That's what Paradise is saying." Mona retorted.

"Paradise would never say that!" Zukie shouted.

The Old Lady stood resolute. Zukie was many things, but a rapist he was not. She at least knew her son that well. This time when she addressed Mrs Browne, there was a threatening edge to her voice.

"If my son do your daughter anyt'ing, call the blasted Police. But don't come 'round yah saying dem t'ings widout proof. If my son is a rapist, mek dem lock him up!"

"We decided not to involve the police." Mona avoided eye contact. "You know that kind of publicity would destroy the church and it wouldn't be in Paradise's best interest. She's young. She made a mistake allowing him in, thinking he could be trusted... Anyway, what is done is done. I have come here to tell you that myself and my husband, out of consideration for you, would like to make an arrangement..."

Mrs Browne stopped in mid-speech and looked across at the church sisters. She motioned to the Old Lady, who resolved that it was time her friends were on their way home. They had enjoyed tea, biscuits, a bit of chit-chat, and enough gossip to last them a month. Despite their vocal protests, she ushered each of them out forcefully, until only she, Zukie and Mrs Browne were left in the hallway.

"As I was saying," Mrs Browne continued, "me and my husband would like to make an arrangement, out of consideration for you... If you are willing to make a donation of £5,000 to the church fund, we would be prepared to forget the whole matter."

The Old Lady's mouth dropped open. She could hardly believe what she was hearing.

"I know what you're thinking," Mona said quickly, "it sounds like a lot of money, but perhaps your other son could help you... You know, the one you're always talking about... the jewellery sales representative who is doing so well."

The Old Lady's mouth was still wide open. Finally, the penny dropped and she exploded.

"Get out, Mona! Get out! Get out! Get out! Get out before I do you somet'ing. You godless, lying, two-faced bitch."

Mona Browne didn't have to be told another time.

The Old Lady's insane look was a warning to make haste. She backed steadily out towards the door and slipped out quickly, only pausing long enough to shout back:

"You'll be sorry... you'll be sorry for this."

The Old Lady slammed the front door shut after her. Then she turned to Zukie.

"And *you*...! Yuh bettah pack yuh bags an' lef'."

GLENN "FLUXY" ELLIS was born into the Seventh Day Adventist Church, and it was his mother's wish that he be buried at the cemetery in Old Trafford. The afternoon was dull and it had been raining ceaselessly.

Glenn's mother, Daisy, a petite woman who was known by her friends as being very proud, was screaming, "Why? Why? Why did he die? Why? Why?" Why her son? Why her baby?

Glenn was lowered into the grave of his father, Thomas. The coffin slipped against the muddy sides of the freshly dug grave. As old time people would say, the duppy was refusing to go down.

His friends huddled around the graveside paying their last respects. Easy-Love, Bluebwai, Teeko and the rotund youth called Slim. He had been their leader. Jigsy couldn't or wouldn't cry. With the black bandanna wrapped around his head, he looked more like a Sikh, but that didn't bother him. He was beside himself with rage and too busy plotting revenge against his brother's killer to shed tears. Storm was going to get fucked up. Jigsy's grief was fury, he wanted blood. If Storm had been at the funeral, he would have dusted him there and then. But first he was going to make Storm suffer as he was suffering. Storm's mother would cry as his mother had cried and still cries. This thing wasn't over. It was only just beginning.

The Piper Mill Crew saluted their fallen leader with a closed fist across their chest, over the heart. They gathered around the grave and raised their fists above their heads in a tight circle. They chanted something Fluxy couldn't hear.

TURNIP, PUMPKIN, POTATOES, okra, green
bananas and a packet of noodles had been left
on the scratched kitchen work top. Storm
touched the pot. It was stone cold. By now Saturday
soup would normally be cooked and ready to serve. He
felt uneasy and for a moment, his deep-set eyes
darkened with worry. It was uncharacteristic of the Old
Lady to start the cooking and leave it unfinished.

His heart stirred. She didn't mention going anywhere
this morning. He took off his leather parka, placing his
portable phone on the kitchen table and depressing the
ignition switch on the front burner. Blue-violet flames
darted from the cast iron pores under the soup pot, and
he felt the instant heat on his face warming him. After a
few minutes, on full heat, the soup started to bubble
gently, sending out a savoury, exotic aroma.

Storm added the rest of the ingredients to the soup
and stared outside. The wind battered against the
kitchen window. Turning from the sink, Storm was
startled by the sight of a body in a black suit lying

crumpled and bloody on the kitchen floor before him. It took another moment for him to realise he was hallucinating.

Storm leaned back on the old chair. Normally nothing troubled him much, but lately things were getting out of control. He was living on a knife's edge and he knew it.

He went back through to the kitchen and picked up his mobile and dialled a number. Lewty's voice came through strong and clear at the other end of the phone.

"Yeah, Lewt, wh'appen?" Clearing his throat, he closed the door with a firm push.

JIGSY SAT HUDDLED in the leather armchair, fingering the trigger of a shiny silver 9mm automatic, his red eyes almost popping with pressure out of their sockets. He was in the apartment he used to share with his brother, Fluxy. Except, he was alone. Fluxy was dead now and buried. Fresh in the grave. The funeral was over.

The spacious apartment was in an old mill warehouse conversion in the Salford Quays complex. It was a big leap from his childhood of poverty and degradation in a grimy block of flats in Moss Side. Despite this, he felt empty, lonely and desperate, and everything hurt. He shouldn't have been in the flat alone, because everything about it reminded him of his dead brother who he missed so badly.

The way Fluxy was murdered in cold blood really cut him up, and it made the Pipers man dem look like shit.

95

He had stayed at home to help his mother get through the pain and heartache leading up to the funeral. Now that was over, it was time to go to work. He had assumed Fluxy's place as leader and things were going to run tight from now on.

Jigsy went through to his kitchen. He was sweating and felt breathless. He needed something to replenish his energy. Pulling the fridge-freezer away from the kitchen wall, he bent down and retrieved the apparatus from its hiding place. He placed it on the kitchen counter. Beads of sweat peeled off his face. Breathing slowly, heavily, he took the cocaine from the small, crumpled brown bag and ground it into a fine, white powder. Sweating profusely now, he put the powder into a bottle and mixed the chemicals. He then put the resulting liquid across a small mirror with an eyedropper. Hands trembling, he dabbed his face with a cloth continuously.

When the liquid dried it left a fine chalky residue. He repeated the process. Almost in a trance he remembered how Fluxy always used to say, 'Sell the stuff, never mess with it!' Fat lot of good that advice did him. Fuck it, Fluxy should have listened to *him*. For the last few months, Jigsy had been telling him that Piper Mill had to move in on the Grange before they moved in on them. You could have seen it coming. Piper Mill's operation was rivalling the Grange's and how long they could exist side by side was anybody's guess, but one thing for sure, one day the one would have to eat up the other. They should have dusted Storm and the whole fucking lot of them when he first suggested it. But Fluxy didn't want to take Storm on and he lost his life because of it.

Like his brother, Jigsy was in the juggling thing deep, but he wasn't in it to lose his life, not unless he was taking a whole heap of people out with him.

He tried to block out his brother's words, 'Sell the stuff, never mess with it'. The residue accumulated until the whole mirror was covered with a thick, white coating and he could no longer see the reflection of his pained, haggard face. He scraped the cocaine off with a razor blade. His heart was racing, his tongue dry.

Placing half a teaspoonful in a pipe, he heated the pipe with his lighter, touching the flame to the powder. He inhaled deeply, groaning. Wiping the mirror quickly, he concealed the works carefully back behind the fridge.

His blood tingled. His brain pleaded. The death of his brother had driven him back to the pipe, back to being a slave to the pipe, when he thought he had given it up.

He headed back into the living room. Light-headed, he sank into the armchair. Still sucking on the pipe, he pulled deeply like it was life-saving oxygen. Oblivion beckoned. Smoke curled into his lungs and carried him floating into another dimension. He rested his eyes for just a second.

When he woke up, his eyes still bloodshot, he knew it was late. He made a phone call. It was time to rally the posse. It was a good night for killing. Storm was going to pay.

THE OLD LADY received the news via Imelda, her sister-in-law, that Vermont had died at two-fifteen in

97

the night. But even before the phone rang she knew it was bad news.

He didn't die peacefully, but in guilt and torment. Oblivious to the presence of his second wife, he had called the pet name of his first wife repeatedly. "Queenie. Queenie. Queenie."

She had denied him the final chance to see the boy. Zukie, the boy he claimed he never knew existed until recently. He had wanted to see the boy so much. Guilt racked her. It was the Old Lady's way of seeking revenge for the pain, misery and distress he had inflicted on her over the past twenty years. If anything, she felt empty. Vermont was gone.

Clifton was asleep downstairs curled up on the settee again when she came down. He was convinced that if he didn't go to sleep, his nightmares couldn't haunt him. But as hard as he tried to stay awake, he always gave in to tiredness. The TV was on with some early morning breakfast show. The gas fire was on full blast and the stale smell of the previous night's drinking and smoking clung to the air. The Old Lady was too grief stricken to curse and complain. She stirred her son awake.

"Me have some bad news to tell you," she wheezed. "Sit up."

"What's up?" Clifton asked. He saw the tears beginning to brim in her eyes.

The Old Lady swallowed deeply, clutching her housecoat tightly. "Yuh Daddy dead. Vermont."

Clifton sighed. He rubbed his eyes and looked into the distance, running a palm backwards across his close-cropped hair. He was reminded about all the things that could have been if his father had been there for him, and if his mother wasn't forced to struggle to bring up her children on her own, when she needed the strength and support of their father around. He knew a lot of people his age who had been raised by one parent and who were now replicating the faults of their parents' generation. He remembered how he had always wanted a father, needed a father. How he had envied those who had fathers they could turn to. How was he supposed to take it after all these years? How could he be expected to suddenly feel like he was the man's son and shed tears for him? That would have been total hypocrisy. The man was living his life somewhere else and wouldn't or couldn't, even once, hear the cry of his woman and pickney. He allowed them to live a life of misery. When Zukie and Clifton were younger, there was never enough money in the house to pay for the essentials, let alone treats. Their father wasn't around when his sons needed loving, and now that he was gone it wouldn't make the slightest impact on his life. As far as Clifton was concerned, the man should have considered that one day his youths were going to grow up and not respect him. They weren't blind and the memory of how their lives used to be without him was still fresh in both their minds. Clifton shrugged his shoulders. He didn't know the man.

"Is that all you woke me up for? Mum, my Dad died a long time ago. So he's dead for real now, so what?"

"Clifton, he give you life, no matter what."

"Look, just don't ask me to go to his funeral."

The Old Lady stared into the emptiness before her, tears streaming down her cheeks.

"I never stop loving him... Try and understand that,

despite whey him do me an' how fe years I tek it cuss him, 'cause it never stop hurting. Despite that, I never stop loving him."

"Yeah, it hurt me too. I'm going back to sleep. I've got things to do later. Life goes on."

ZUKIE WAS IN love. He had never felt this way before but there was no mistaking it, this was what the poets called love. He went through his days with Paradise on his mind. He couldn't tell if it was morning or afternoon, early or late, or whether he was sad or happy. He had found the woman that he wanted, rich in beauty, intelligent and strong, yet he didn't have her. He had totally lost himself. This wasn't the Zukie that he recognised, but some other romantic. What if she really had told her parents that he raped her? What then? Wasn't that the cold reality of their relationship? She was out to save her own skin. He cursed himself for having such thoughts. Paradise wouldn't do that to him. He could feel that. He was sure she liked him as much as he liked her, and she was thinking about him right now.

He hadn't been able to get in touch with her since that fateful night, when her father and brothers returned home early and intruded upon them. He had made several telephone calls to her house but only her father or mother answered, never Paradise. When her parents heard his voice they would replace the receiver. He had only been bold enough to knock on the door once, and at that time the Pastor came after him with a baseball bat and threatened to call the police if he didn't kill him first. Zukie didn't turn around to take in the murderous look on the Pastor's face, but legged it down the road as niftily as his legs would carry him. There was a time for everything and right now didn't seem like the right time to anger the Pastor any further.

He had even spent hours standing across the road from her house, hiding in the bushes, keeping a watch, waiting to see if he could get a glimpse of her. Even though he stood watching her room all night, he never saw her once. He even made some enquiries and found out which college she attended and asked around there, but nobody had seen her for several days. One of her friends told him that she had gone away for a few weeks, but Zukie was still suspicious. Why had she not tried to contact him? Why all the mystery?

Since the Old Lady threw him out, Zukie had been crashing on Chico's floor at his mother's place on Claremont Road. It was a temporary arrangement, which suited Zukie fine. He didn't need too much space and the contribution of £10 a week expected from him was exactly what he could afford. Through a friend of a friend, he had even managed to get a few days work, painting and decorating for a Housing Association in the area. It wasn't much, but it was cash in hand and it helped out.

"Zukie! Zukie!"

Zukie turned to the sound of a female voice calling

him from across the road. Even though she hadn't seen him in a while and his work clothes and face were splashed with white paint and his trademark sandy dreadlocks were completely hidden in a red, green and gold tam, she recognised him immediately. He recognised her, too. It was Marie. It was a while since he last saw his first girlfriend. She was pushing her daughter, Candy, in a pushchair.

He crossed the busy road, side-stepping the traffic to the blare of angry horns. "Marie, wha' happen? How's things?" Bending down, he kissed Candy, a beautiful dark-skinned child. "You're not shy are you, Candy?" he teased. "You know who this is, don't you?"

The little child looked at Zukie, bewildered.

"She's the image of you," Zukie stated. Marie smiled.

"You look criss," Zukie said, taking a step back to admire Marie's new weave. "Yeah, it really suits you. So how yuh keepin'?"

"I wish I felt as good as you say I look," marie said with a sigh.

Zukie nodded understandingly. He knew exactly what she meant. He reached into a back pocket for his wallet and produced a fiver and bent down to give it to Candy.

"Uncle Zukie's got a little present for you," he said, tucking the money gently into the child's tiny fur duffle coat. "That's for being a good little girl."

The child continued looking at him, bewildered, and then looked down at the money sticking out of her coat, then back to Zukie, but could not make head or tail out of it.

"No, Zukie, you can't do that," Marie said quickly.

"Whe' yuh mean? She's like my niece. Is not every day me see her."

Candy wasn't his niece, not in the true sense. Within a few months of breaking up with Zukie, Marie got herself a new boyfriend and got pregnant. Marie was a mother at sixteen. Candy's father didn't hang around long and, when the responsibilities of fatherhood came crashing down before him, he suddenly decided he was too young and wanted to be independent like before.

Zukie still cared about Marie and knew that life as a single mother wasn't easy and he often helped her out financially with what little he had, whenever he bumped into her.

"It's not charity, Marie. It's love. And don't tell me, money can't buy love."

Marie looked down into her daughter's pushchair. "I wouldn't know..." They became momentarily silent.

"When was the last time you saw baby father?" Zukie asked.

"Yesterday."

"How is he?"

"Fine."

Zukie studied Marie's tired eyes closely. It didn't matter how many times he urged her to forget her baby father, he sensed that she was still in love with the wrong man. That was her initial downfall, and she seemed to be continuing in the same vein.

"I know..." she conceded quietly. "I should just carry on my life without him, but it in't that easy, Zukie. Candy is part of him too... It's so difficult to let go."

"You shouldn't let him play around with you, he isn't worth it," Zukie stressed.

"You're still sore about it, aren't you?"

"Sore?" Zukie smiled. He was sore at the time when she ditched him for a sweetbwai. But that was a long time ago. Now, with the girl he had once held a torch for in front of him, he couldn't be sore. She was still beautiful. A beautiful girl tied and chained to the wrong man.

"Where you going, Marie?"

Marie took a deep breath.

"I'm going home. I got a flat just down the bottom of this road. You should come by some time."

She called out the number of her house as she made her way on, pushing the pram before her. Zukie called back that he would definitely drop by some time.

"DADDY! DADDY! DAAAADDDEEE!!" The young boy was playing out on the pavement in front of his house with some friends. He was the smallest boy of the group, but had the biggest ears and the widest smile. His older female admirers usually described him as "cute". When the boy noticed the tall man with sunglasses step out of the gleaming black car, he dropped what he was doing, abandoned his friends, and screamed excitedly as he ran.

Clifton looked up quickly, slamming the door of his car, a frown fading from his face. As the boy rushed to him, he scooped his son up, holding him tightly.

"Lee, Lee, Lee!" He called the boy's name over and over again. He lifted the laughing child high above his head. Then held him close again. He touched the boy's neck gently with his lips. He had missed not being able to hug his son, to touch him, smell him, hear him. He had missed Lee so much. He could feel Lee's chest begin to heave rapidly. He lifted his son's head. Lee started to cry, racking his body with sobs.

"Lee, what's wrong?" his father asked anxiously. "What is it, baby?"

Lee clung to his father's neck tight, like his life depended on it and continued sobbing.

"Come on Lee, talk to Daddy. What's wrong?"

The four-year-old boy drew his head back slowly. He looked very fair in the daylight, his hair a mass of loose black curls, his brown eyes wide and filled with grief. He peered into his Daddy's face, staring intensely.

"Where've you been, Daddy? I missed you. Where were you?"

Clifton felt the blood draining from his face and a panic rising out of the pit of his stomach. He didn't know what to say. Instead, still carrying his son, he went to the boot of his car, opened it and watched his son's eyes light up at the sight of the brand new, red BMX bike wrapped in cellophane.

"Is that for me?" the boy asked enthusiastically. His father had only started to nod his head when the boy shouted, "Yippee!" He hugged his father's neck and kissed him.

"Put me down... I wanna ride it now."

His father obliged and put the boy down. He pulled the bike out of the boot and removed the cellophane. His son could hardly wait. Clifton watched proudly as Lee rode cautiously along the pavement.

"Just don't go near the road!" he called after him.

With a nod, the boy promised he wouldn't.

He found her in the living room, lying on the sofa, surrounded by books. As usual, her hair was styled in twists rather than plaits. She looked studious with her oversize glasses resting on the tip of her nose. She always seemed to look even prettier when she was studying, Clifton reflected. Her pencil-thin eyebrows would arch when she was concentrating as she was now, and make her hazel eyes seem larger and more innocent. Fully consumed by what she was reading, Jasmine was oblivious to his presence.

"Jazzy?"

She jumped up, startled. Flicking the long twists off her face, she faced Clifton for the first time in months. She was almost as tall as he was so there eyes met at the same level. He swallowed painfully, as he saw the negative expression on her face. Seconds passed as they stood gazing at each other, he nervously twisting the stud in his ear.

They were both too young when Jazzy gave birth to Lee. They were children having children, but somehow they managed to cope and, even though he spent a lot of time away from his responsibilities, things would have probably turned out alright if Jazzy had remained ignorant of the reality of the life Clifton was living. It must have been a year ago now. They were driving to the City Centre, in the Audi Clifton used to have, to do some Christmas shopping. It was only late afternoon, but it was already dark, and Christmas lights illuminated everywhere. They had been discussing which presents to surprise Lee with on Christmas Day, as they waited for the lights to change to green. Out of nowhere, two men appeared, their identities hidden by the ski masks on their faces. At the same instant, the windscreen shattered into a million pieces as it was struck by a baseball bat. Then the side window. Then the windscreen caved in. Jasmine screamed, hysterical, and Storm finally stomped the gas pedal, sending the car forward in a screech of burning tyre rubber.

All his explanations did no good. Jasmine was adamant.

"Cliff, I can't live like this," she said plaintively. Clifton asked for understanding. Jasmine asked for a closer relationship, a better life. She didn't want his life to put her in danger. It was clear to Cliff that if they could not reach a common ground, they would grow further apart. He wanted to understand her fears, but he was under stress himself, the stress of a man who knew there were people out there who, given the chance, would kill him. It exhausted him. The gulf between them inevitably widened. Jazzy made it clear that if he didn't give up the gang thing, she would put him behind her and forget their relationship ever happened.

Wearing a pair of battered blue jeans and one of Cliff's sweatshirts several sizes too big for her, Jasmine parted her trembling lips and let out a fragile sigh. She wanted to run across to him, but she felt too bitter.

"Finally decide to show your face?" she snapped.

"Jazz," he took a step forward, ignoring her uninviting welcome. "How you been keeping?"

"Why don't you ask Lee?" she said bitterly. "Ask him

how we've been keeping, or how he's been feeling."

"Hey, I come in peace!" Cliff said, trying to lighten her up. He saw from the scowl on her face that she was unimpressed.

"Okay, if I'm not welcome..." he began, turning to go.

"You haven't even been here two minutes and you're ready to go!" Jazzy called after. "Two minutes, you think that's going to make up for all the time Lee's been without his father?"

He stopped dead in his tracks. Trying to control his rapid breathing, he turned. At the same time his mobile phone rang. For a moment he didn't know what to do, then he decided to answer it. It was Lewty.

"Not right now, Lewty. I'm dealing with my woman. Later."

He snapped the phone shut and pressed the power button to 'off'. He walked back to Jasmine, feeling helpless.

"I'm dealing with my woman!" Jazzy echoed angrily. "What do you mean by that exactly?"

"Just cool, Jazz. You know I didn't mean anything by that. It's just lyrics that's all. There's no need to take offence."

"So I'm your woman now am I? After all this time away, you still think you have a right to refer to me as your woman? You gotta be joking. Where were you Clifton? We needed you to be near us. We needed you with us. You've been gone for a year."

Clifton was unable to respond.

She brushed the twists of her face slowly with the back of her hand. "You never want to talk about anything, Cliff." Dark shadows were under her eyes. She started to cry. Her nose and mascara were running. "Why did you let this happen to us? We were beautiful together, once."

Cliff knew she was right.

"I'm sorry."

Storm looked up at the ceiling. His head felt like it was about to explode. "I'm really sorry, Jazzy."

For some reason Jasmine laughed.

Clifton was serious. He really was sorry, sorry that he had chosen his crew over his family. He wanted to tell her that things would change, but how could he? How would things change? How would things be different? He pondered the thought for a moment. He could offer to move to Stretford, or even Stockport, like Jazzy always used to suggest. But not now, not right now. He reached over to her and pulled her protectively to his chest.

Later that night, she would regret having allowed Clifton back into her bed, convinced that he would disappear after a night. But she hadn't protested when he silenced her resistance with a kiss. She said nothing as he lifted her off her feet and eased her down on the bed, and she simply lay back with her eyes closed when he lifted up her jumper and caressed her nipple with his tongue.

"Mmmmn...." she sighed, urging him to continue.

Slipping out of his trousers, Clifton positioned himself between Jazzy's legs. She wrapped them firmly around his waist, pulling him in, and as he entered, she gripped his behind and cried, "Yes, yes... oh Clifton. Yes!"

Yes, he was back in her life, but Clifton knew it was

110

not to be. He would stay for a night, or maybe two. He didn't want to lose Jazzy, but things couldn't go back to the way they had been. His life was complicated enough already.

THE PROUD FATHER cradled his tiny daughter. He was in the maternity wing of the hospital, in the small room Lalah shared with three other women. Those women also had their family members with them, all admiring the new babies the mothers had brought into the world. But Cliff was the proudest man in the room.

"She's nothing like you," he teased as he rocked his baby gently. "Look at her nose, her mouth. She's my mirror image exactly."

Lalah simply frowned. Though she was small in size, she was strong-willed and tough. But she had now been kept in the hospital for several days. She was tired and wanted to go home, but the doctors were waiting for the results of tests. They wanted to be sure that both mother and child were doing well before they released her. They didn't allay her fears. However, she was promised that they would be able to go home tomorrow. She couldn't wait.

Cliff looked proudly down at his daughter, tears

almost coming to his eyes. She was so tiny and looked so vulnerable, so dependant on him. He had never seen a baby that small. He held her even closer. Her little eyes staring up at him.

Before he knew it visiting hours were over and he kissed Lalah goodbye. He'd try and come back the next day.

T HE CRUSHED EMPTY cigarette packet hit the
gutter as Storm stepped out of his new BMW
parked on double yellow lines outside the
bank in Spring Gardens, Manchester City Centre.
Compared to Moss Side, the place was like a breath of
fresh air. Everywhere was crisp, new, clean and
gleaming. Like a different town, far away from the
ghetto. He was thinking of Rough Cut.

There was nothing he could do for Rough Cut. It was
all down to the doctors now. But every other member of
the posse was crying out for revenge. Storm knew what
he would do, but it had to wait until after the concert.
Tonight they were going to make some money and have
a roadblock dance. Storm felt the cold wind biting
through his leather parka. Thrusting his hands deep
inside his pockets, he rushed into the bank, through the
automatic doors, welcoming the warmth from the
heating vents above the door.

He was there to make a large withdrawal. The Shabba
Ranks showcase that evening was a Grange promotion.

It was bound to be rammed with ravers, but he needed money upfront to pay the artists.

The bank's security guard eyed him suspiciously as he took his place in the queue. Storm smiled at him. He walked up to the cashier, conscious of the camera above. He handed over the signed cheque. The cashier asked him the usual.

"Do you have any identification?" Storm was used to it. The bank however, were not used to young black men drawing out large sums of money. Apparently, Mr Michaels was a concert promoter, which explained his sizeable deposits and withdrawals. Storm produced his driving licence and then watched interestedly as the cashier went off to make her checks and then return to her window.

He watched her carefully, as she counted the notes. Shabba Ranks' manager had warned them that his artist wasn't going to sing a note unless he got paid in full, in advance.

THE SHABBA RANKS' concert at the Carib Club was proving to be a big success, and at 12:40, the club's management decided to temporarily close the front doors. The club was already too full.

An angry crowd started to gather, inching their way towards the doors, frantically waving twelve pound admission tickets. An early morning police patrol car slithered by like a snake in the darkness, the two policemen inside the unit surveying the scene absently.

It picked up speed and was gone.

Ten minutes later the club doors were re-opened and ticket holders started to ease their way inside.

At about the same time, three black BMW's with darkened windows drove into the area of the club. Two of the cars blocked the road in either direction, and the other car eased into the front of the car park. None of the vehicles had registration plates.

Security at the club was inefficient, only one man with a walkie-talkie on patrol outside. Walking with a pronounced swagger, the young security guard was more interested in the amount of 'fitness' coming to the dance. He bit into his sandwich and munched with a big smile on his face. The sight of a dark BMW with tinted windows idling near the entrance to the car park caught his eye. Maybe, he thought to himself, the car was part of Shabba Ranks' extensive entourage. He judged it okay for it to enter the restricted artists' entrance, but first walked over to the driver's side. The electric window slid down slowly. The next thing he saw was a small, black revolver pointing in his face. His heart pumping like a piston and his mind racing with fear, the guard wet himself. A cool voice ordered him to relax. One of the passengers stepped out of the car and prodding the guard forward with a gun, forced him into the car with them.

At the club's front doors a young, black man in an expensive designer suit started arguing with one of the doormen.

"Because I haven't got a ticket, I have to pay fifteen pounds?!" The youth was shouting. A vein in his temple pumped visibly. "Why should I? The show has already fucking started!"

"Well, you should have been here earlier," the burly doorman calmly remarked. He wasn't bothered by the youth's attitude. He was the beefiest bouncer at the place. Everybody knew he could take care of himself, he didn't have to prove anything.

"What?" the youth retorted, incensed as the doorman allowed some people with tickets to pass. "You mean I should have camped outside the fucking doors in the rain? What's wrong with you man? I was here earlier and the queue was as long and as wide as the inside of your wife's pussy."

The doorman looked at the young funki dred. He was sure he'd seen this face before.

"Don't get personal with me. If you don't want to pay, well, that's fine, just step aside. There are plenty of people with tickets and the money."

"Yeaaahhh?!" the youth drawled, a strange grin appearing on his face. "You must be making it tonight, eh? Must be running into thousands already, eh...? Well, I'll tell you who I am, motherfucker!"

Instinct told the doorman that something wasn't quite right. Something was about to happen. He broke into a cold sweat. Suddenly, three more men appeared, their faces hidden behind large handkerchiefs and bandannas. All three held semi-automatic weapons. All the guns were aimed at him.

He now knew what was going down. But it was too late. Like a bad dream in slow motion, time froze for the doorman. He saw the large, automatic Colt .45 appear from the inside of the grinning youth's jacket. Easy-Love. Now he remembered. Wasn't that what they called him? He remembered Easy-Love from a previous argument where he was forced to back down. Wasn't he Piper Mill? This time he couldn't take the youth on without back-up. The doorman turned to call for assistance. The scene that greeted him was a siege. Turning back, he saw the blue fire from the gun. Half of his body appeared to shut down. He saw people fleeing in all directions. Screams filled his head. Screams, noises, music. Then he could no longer hear, no longer see, no longer feel. He gave in to the dark, cold blanket wrapping him. He fell to the ground with a sickening thud. The harder they come, the harder they fall.

Easy jumped over the doorman's body and grabbed a young dark-skinned girl in a blonde wig. He dug the Colt .45 into her cheek and twisted her left arm up behind her back, until her wrist snapped. The girl screamed in agony. In the melee, her wig slipped off, revealing a short, relaxed hair style underneath. Easy thought she looked even more attractive now, and felt his cock wriggle to life as he brushed his groin against the girl's buttocks.

"What's your name?" He demanded from the petrified girl.

The young teenager's eyes rolled round in their sockets, as if possessed by a demon. Saliva dripped from the sides of her painted lips, mingling with the tears on her chin. "Let me go! Please, please, let me go!" she pleaded.

The other three gunmen pointed their handguns at the other bouncers standing paralysed at their posts.

"I said what's your fucking name?!" Easy was becoming a little agitated.

"Marianne," she spluttered. Her tongue felt heavy.

"Marianne, sorry about this. But one wrong move from anybody and I'm afraid Marianne, you're dead. Hey you stupid, ugly bastards!" he shouted at the bouncers. "One wrong move and Marianne here, won't be here, got it?!" He chuckled, his eyes wild with cocaine-induced fire. "And all that cash you've made on the door, we want it. Now! Still in the cash bags. No tricks. Move!!!"

"Alright, alright boy, tek it easy."

"Don't call me no fucking bwai! That's what I told him!" He waved the gun at the doorman lying in a heap, a steady flow of blood trickling out of him. "Get dealing with the readies or you'll end up like him!"

One of the other gunmen, a huge, big-bellied youth, moved forward. "Easy, man, take it easy, stay calm." He turned the doorman over with the tip of his foot. "Why'd you have to hit him, anyway?"

"Fuck you, Slim!" Easy responded. "I'll do him how I feel like. You don't like it, go stick your head up your arse. I already tell you, he called me a 'bwai'. I'm no boy, I'm the man!"

"Looks like he's dead."

Easy grinned, shrugging his shoulders. "Well, there in't nowt you can do for him, is there?"

The other bouncers were busy pushing loose notes into small cloth bags. They finished quickly, and two of the gunmen filled a large holdall with the cash bags. The other two had their guns trained on the bouncers, but they weren't about to get any heroics from the club's security team. Having witnessed the bloody sight of their colleague's bullet-punctured body, and the madness that these gunmen could wreak, they thought it best to behave themselves.

Four more gunmen came in from outside. The gang moved through the foyer and into the dancehall.

In a private room near the top balcony, word of the robbery reached the three Grange members. It took only half a minute for everyone to check their weapons and make their way down.

Shabba, the Grammy Award winner, Mister Loverman, was performing his best tonight. It was the fourth leg of his U.K. tour and he liked the vibes coming from the crowd, all that wild enthusiastic screaming. He was in favour of the special gunshot effects, so he bounced about on the stage enjoying the euphoria:

"Ding-a-ling-a-ling...school bell ah ring...knife an' fork ah fight fe gun t'ing......"

The Pipers licked a barrage of shots into the ceiling. Panic gripped the crowd. The audience weren't screaming for Shabba now, but for their lives. A couple of youths near one of the exit doors suddenly produced guns and returned fire. Most people dived to the grimy, wet floor, but some stood still, rooted to the spot, frozen by terror.

Shabba was quickly hustled off the stage by his personal security, as the promoter dived to take cover. The band needed no urging to do the same.

Miraculously, no one was killed in the ensuing battle. Survivors would later insist that this was only due to divine intervention. At the sound of police sirens in the distance, the gunmen seemed to disappear into thin air.

THE POLICE DECIDED it was time for a crack down. A convoy of police vans and cars moved slowly into the area of the Piper Mill pub to support the foot patrol. Even at this hour, their presence was detected by a hooded Piper streetboy on his mountain bike, doing his early morning surveillance rounds on the estate, equipped with a pair of powerful binoculars.

And the cry went up into the dawn sky.

"Beast! Dibbles!! Beast! Beastbwai!!" A couple of other boys on similar bikes fled the area. Picking up speed with the wind, their voices carrying the cry into the area.

"Police! Beastbwai!!!"

Within minutes an increasingly large number of youths had gathered, some still bleary-eyed from a rude awakening, taking up a confrontational stance towards the police who had now saturated the estate. The youths teased and cajoled them, laughing as the police made their way through the estate systematically, pounding in doors where they thought they might find something, and cross-checking the ownership of cars parked in the area.

The raid led to the arrest of a handful of criminals, the seizure of a couple of ounces of cannabis resin and a handgun. It was a disappointing tally, but as far as the police were concerned it was better than nothing and sufficient justification for their heavy-handed tactics.

The raids continued through the entire day and night. Throughout Manchester, clubs, shebeens and blues were targeted, as well as a number of private houses in areas as far apart as Cheetham Hill, Whalley Range and Old Trafford. At all these places, the police found their pickings slim. By the end of the operation, more than one officer voiced their suspicions that a good number of people had been tipped off in advance.

THE OLD LADY dusted down the oversize black two-piece from her wardrobe. She hated wearing it because she only took it out whenever someone died. Even though it was expected, she still hadn't quite got over Vermont's death. To lose someone you had been through so much with was one thing, but to lose him without having had the chance to forgive and forget was painful. She felt guilty. Why had she so stubbornly refused him his wish to see his sons before he died? It seemed to make sense at the time; the boys had done well enough all these years without a father, and she didn't want them to go through the pain of finding and then losing a father they had never known. Wasn't that the reason? Why did it now seem like such an irrelevant matter of principle? She sighed. Even in death, Vermont had such a power over her thoughts and morality, as he had done during their marriage.

Vermont came to the UK first, from their sunny home in the Caribbean in the late sixties, looking for work.

Streets paved with gold, they had said. He arrived on that winter's day all those years ago to find that the streets were paved with cold slabs of concrete, and the British people had a coldness and a greyness to match. Still, he made the best he could out of the situation and struggled through regardless. Queenie joined her husband two years later, and she got a job at a hospital. Vermont, a man not unlike many of his generation, had worked in factories, shops, and stores, as well as dug ditches and planted trees, work which allowed for food, clothes and housing.

From as early as she could remember, people had called her Queenie. They said that, even as a baby, she had held her head proudly and of course, she was christened Henrietta after a European Queen. She left school at the age of fourteen after a colonial education amounting to little more than knowing the three R's and that England was the Mother of the Empire and fortunately God was on her side. After school she got a job in a nursing home near her village of Bluefields, in Westmoreland, helping to look after the sick and elderly. It was there she met her future husband, Vermont, when he came to visit an elderly relative. Vermont's light-tan complexion placed him in a category in Jamaican society to which a very black girl with no money and without a good profession, like Queenie, didn't belong. On his grandfather's side, he descended from white aristocracy who had once owned a plantation. Even though his family objected strongly to the match, Vermont was determined to win the hand of his 'Queen' in marriage. She willingly moved from country to town to be with him.

It wasn't long before Queenie gave birth to their first child, a girl who they named Grace. Even though they had to live frugally on Vermont's small clerk's salary from the Kingston bank, they were able to rent a small government apartment on the Spanish Town Road. It was a modest dwelling, even by Kingstonian standards. It had two rooms and a tiny kitchen. They continued to live there even after their sons, Neville and Phillip, were born.

The young family were very happy during this time. They didn't have much money, but they were determined that their children would live an easier life than they had lived. Increasingly, it became clear that things weren't going to change for them very much in Jamaica. This was the age of mass emigration from the island. All around them friends and family were departing for the prosperous climes of New York, Miami, Toronto and Britain, and returning home to Jamaica on holidays with stories of high wages and lives of luxury. With every day that passed, more and more people crossed the seas, to take work at any price.

Eventually, they saved enough money for Vermont to sail to England. He had no problems entering this country, because his grandfather was British. This was still the late-sixties and it would take two more years before Queenie herself was able to join her husband in Manchester. They decided to leave the children in Jamaica with their paternal grandparents, to finish off their education. Even now, Queenie regretted that she had little contact with her eldest children, apart from the occasional letter or telephone call. Grace was now living in Toronto, while Philip and Neville both emigrated to the United States to live in Texas and New York respectively.

Queenie arrived in England with ten pounds in her pocket. She found her husband still living in a bedsit and working night and day to make ends meet, having discovered that life for new immigrants was not as rosy as had been painted back home. He burned paraffin for heating, because he couldn't afford gas or electricity, and he still seemed to be doing what seemed to her like menial jobs. By Caribbean standards, they nevertheless lived well. Except this wasn't the Caribbean. There were those who did worse over there, and in Britain there were many who did better and had more, much more.

It was difficult to adjust to each other after an absence of two years. When his wife arrived to join him, Vermont expected to embrace her, and kiss her, and love her after such a long time. And in those days she was so slim, one of his arms could slip around her waist to hold her close to him. He had gone over all he wanted to say to her in his head, rehearsed it thoroughly. But now she was there, he was lost for words. He cursed England. He felt ashamed by what he saw as his failure and inability to have succeeded in the few years he had spent overseas. Since arriving on British shores, he had known that stinging taste of bitterness which comes with having to deal on a day to day basis with the stench of small-minded people at work and out of work. Only the weekends offered some small relief from the treadmill, because he would go to The Club, where he could forget the factory and the strange accents asking foolish questions. At The Club, he could be amongst his people, just plain, raw Caribbean people, meeting each other, greeting each other, fighting each other, cursing each other, shouting at each other, and competing with each other.

It was always their intention to send for the children as soon as they were more settled. But one thing led to another and they never managed to bring them across. Vermont and Queenie came to England to 'make something' of themselves. With very little money and no real home to talk of, they would be bringing their children into worse conditions than they were living in at the moment. They decided it was best if their children completed their education in Jamaica, by then Vermont and his wife would certainly have managed to settle down in a proper home to welcome their children to. Meanwhile, Queenie wrote to her children at least once a week. Her letters never quite said what she wanted them to say. She felt she could never express her true feelings and how much she missed them. But however much they tried to save money, the tax man or some other debt collector would take it even faster. Finally, Queenie wrote to tell her children that they now had a younger brother.

With the new baby on its way, and having just lost his job in the biscuit factory, Vermont started taking on jobs as a handyman, doing odd jobs, and advertising: 'no job too small'. He hung wallpaper and doors, he painted, laid carpets and did just about anything he was called to do. He didn't earn much and sometimes it was barely enough, but he was his own boss. He'd had so many bad jobs over those other years that he found the independence suited him. At one time, Vermont wanted more for himself and his family and always believed that he could have it simply through work, but no matter what he did, that route was always difficult. They had to scrimp and save, and Vermont constantly had to discipline himself by remembering how his parents lived back home, and teaching himself to appreciate what little he did have. For his children, he wanted to offer more. He bought an assortment of clothes and toys for his son. He denied his wife nothing, even though she was a woman who asked for little. For himself, he was happy to have work clothes and T-shirts necessary for his jobs, and one nice suit, with a pair of patent leather boots for Sundays and special occasions.

Even though he was content with just making a living, he needed to invest in what was now becoming a lucrative little earner. He purchased tools and materials and eventually managed to buy a second hand van. It would enable him to take on more work. Together with Queenie's salary from the hospital, they would be able to afford that other child they had talked about to keep little Clifton company. Queenie had been so proud of her husband and, even though she dreamt of going back to her home in Jamaica, with things looking better for them every day, she finally came to realise that her family were going to stay in Britain for a while.

The Old Lady stared into space with gap-toothed wonderment, past memories travelling through her like a spirit, haunting gently about her soul. Tears from those doleful eyes threatening to extinguish the etchings from her mind. She wanted to make those memories go away. They always made her long for Vermont, those demons from the past, those dreams of her man on a white horse. She wanted to forget them, because those memories wore the clothes of despair and breathed the air of pain and disappointment.

Almost despite herself, she recalled the good times, when it looked like they were going to make it. Vermont's little business was doing well and they were able to enjoy themselves for the first time. Vermont's sister was in England and lived not too far away with her family, and was only too happy to babysit her nephew when Vermont and Queenie went out at the weekend. They would go out dancing. At the time, the many shebeens were still the best and cheapest places to have a good time. Clubs like the old Sphinx and the Vegas, out on Princess Road used to draw a decent crowd until their clientele changed and rudies took over the place. That's why Vermont and Queenie and most of their friends started going dancing at the church hall on Monton Street instead. The Sphinx and the Vegas were gone now, demolished. Advertising boards now stand on the derelict wasteland where they once stood. Not only did they service their customers with music from back home, but the entrepreneurial men and women who ran them always made sure that there was a list of supplies and refreshments from back home to make their clients feel comfortable. Queenie remembered how towards morning, the menfolk used to gather in the tiny kitchen to share a warm bottle of rum in paper cups, exchanging smiles and silences between themselves in a secret solidarity. From Monday to Friday they would work for 'the Man', but the weekend was theirs, and they knew it. Some of these shebeens would even feature an impromptu live jam session with a local young musician with a hot little band. If their timing was right, Vermont and Queenie would jump out of a cab late at night, and dash quickly into their favourite dance, and arrive in time to hear the live spot preaching into a tenor saxophone or testifying the bass. Shoulders back and eyes rolled back, Vermont would hold his wife tight across the waist — and oh, her waist was so slim then — and escort her in a soft-shoe shuffle in the cramped and darkened room with the other couples there. Queenie and Vermont had a special love and she never, in her wildest dreams, thought it would go away. She never imagined that in just another year, it would be all over. And she never thought that Vermont would die so relatively young, and that she would be sitting dusting off her mourning clothes to wear at his funeral. Vermont had been her best friend, her soul brother, as well as her husband. She could talk to him so easily and told him all her feelings. He always understood and helped her get through her low points.

Then one day Vermont's van was stolen, with all his tools and equipment inside. Desperate, Vermont pestered the police to send out a major search party to look for it, but they declined. Worse still, the insurance company were refusing to pay on some minor technicality to do with him forgetting to sign his insurance papers, and not sending them back in time. Vermont was shattered, and for weeks walked around in a daze, unable almost to even look at his wife whose sole income was what was keeping the family alive. There was a huge strain between them. That's when she was diagnosed with asthma for the first time and started using an inhaler. Queenie urged her husband to get off his backside and get any kind of job. Vermont read that as meaning that she was ashamed of him for failing in his ventures, as ashamed as he himself was. She tried to convince him otherwise, but he insisted, and spent the days moping about his predicament rather than trying to get some money together. Eventually, he couldn't take his wife's looks and silent moments any longer and picked himself up to go to the pub with some mates. He never came back home.

It was funny how sometimes the Old Lady could see Vermont in Zukie. The father he had never known had left his mark on his younger son. In Zukie's eyes she saw the same silent pride which had forced his father to abandon his family, rather than pick himself up after his distress, dust himself down and start all over again.

Well, Vermont was dead now, his body asleep, his mind at rest. Outside the sky darkened and a slight drizzle fell from the skies. The Old Lady turned towards the bedroom window. For a moment she watched the little black girls in front of her house, with their shiny knees and African hair styles, playing a skipping game. Mesmerised by the magic in their fast feet, she thought, these children are future stars. Suddenly, she heard the roar of a powerful engine and saw the car pull up. Clifton climbed out. Her son was now driving a different sleek, black car, with darkened windows. The Old Lady didn't know anything about cars, but even she could tell that it was expensive. Clifton had to be doing really well in his job for him to keep getting such nice company cars, she concluded. She watched as he slammed the driver's door hard and locked it with his remote control, before making his way up the path.

"I been calling you," he said, as he entered his mother's bedroom. The Old Lady read beyond the concern, something like hurt and fear rolled into one. "I thought you weren't in."

"If I'm not here, I'm at work. You know that." She sounded irritated.

"You okay?" he asked.

"Not really," she answered.

"You thinking about the funeral?" he asked quietly. He felt nervous and helpless.

"Me not too sure if me want to go to your father's funeral 'pon me own. Yuh know with all those family me nuh see fe years. Then there's his new wife an all ah her family..."

There was a long pause. Clifton shifted about uneasily. There were still a few days to go until the funeral, but there were a lot of things to do and he didn't have the time. Things like funerals tended to take a lot of time. Somehow, he realised he had no choice.

"I'll be there with you, Mum," he said finally. "I won't let you go alone. Zukie'll come too. I'll make sure he shows his face."

"I loved that man," the Old Lady muttered to herself.

"I know." Clifton didn't want the Old Lady to cry. He couldn't take that right now.

"Men don't know what love is," she said. And then absentmindedly, "Vermont ah sleep now and the whole of we still tired like a raas..." She sat down on her bed and sighed.

Clifton felt as though his spirit was trying to flee his tormented mind. It had been a heavy night. Pure helicopter and t'ing and road blocks. He had only just made it through and driven out of the city to lie low overnight. But a dozen or so youths from various areas had been rounded up.

"You not listening to me." The Old Lady's voice penetrated his thoughts.

"What?"

The Old Lady stared at him with widening eyes. "Yuh have a black suit fe the funeral?"

R EGRETS? HE WASN'T a person to experience these feelings often. He had to be strong. He couldn't, wouldn't, allow himself to be haunted by regrets. Jigsy sighed frustratingly. But he couldn't allow himself to forget. That bastard Storm was to blame for all of this. If he didn't have to reflect on it so much, it wouldn't hurt him so bad. But it did. The truth was he did have regrets.

He had always had regrets, from the moment he was born. He wasn't as tall as his elder brother, wasn't as good at sports, and was never as attractive to the women. Most importantly, he wasn't as sharp as his brother. Fluxy had been the clever one, even when they were at school. Yeah, Jigsy thought to himself, only the good die young.

All of a sudden he wanted to cry. He hadn't wept at all at his brother's funeral, but now it hit him that Fluxy was gone forever, never going to come back. Now here he was, wanting to sit down in the darkness and weep all the troubled waters out of his body. He couldn't remember the last time he cried, long forgotten its therapeutic value. Like Mum always says, the purpose of shedding tears is to purge your soul, to release it, to wash away your torment. Torment. The right word. His mind teased him that Fluxy was dead and buried, and yet Jigsy's burning thirst for revenge was still unquenched.

He searched around for the tiny piece of rock which had fallen somewhere on the deep pile carpet. He surprised himself when he found it, and shouted out with rejoicing as he held it up to the light: "Yes! Yes!" He kissed the cocaine and laughed out aloud with triumphant, deranged laughter. "Ketch you now, yuh raas!!"

CLIFF, WAKE UP!" He heard the voice call somewhere in his subconscious. Words were spinning like a merry-go-round in his head, a kaleidoscope of sentences. "It's me, Lalah, it's me."

It was still morning visiting hours. A pretty, blonde nurse was standing by the doorway to Lalah's room. She smiled, checking that everything was alright, before she continued about her business.

He was sitting on a chair. He looked up at Lalah lying in her bed beside him, her short, boyish haircut and her small size sometimes made her look like a pixie. He was so tired he had fallen asleep in the middle of a conversation with her. He couldn't remember falling into the journey of the unknown, but it took him somewhere he didn't want to go. Fluxy's territory. His stiff neck served to remind him that it hadn't been a very comfortable dream.

Lalah stared at him with a determined look on her face.

"How comes you're so tired?" she asked. "Haven't you been getting enough sleep lately?"

Storm rose unsteadily, as if walking on a thin piece of wire, balancing precariously a hundred feet up. He stretched his arms wide and yawned. This was the third day in a row that he had been at the hospital. After spending so little time at his baby mother's bedside, he was feeling guilty and trying his best to do the right thing as a father, while trying to juggle the rest of his life as well.

"Yeah, you know, the runnings and all..."

There was no way he could tell her what was really on his mind, what his response to the stick-up at the Shabba concert should be. He desperately needed to figure out a way of avoiding full-scale war.

"Keeps you up all night, does it?" Lalah asked.

Storm couldn't make out whether she really was interested or not. He looked at her closely, but couldn't tell.

"Yeah, most nights. Even when I switch off the mobile, people seem able to reach me."

"Eh? That's not possible?" Lalah said.

"You're telling me it's not."

Storm had come to the hospital early, because they were supposed to be going home today. The baby was still asleep when he got there, but awoke shortly after with a dangerously high temperature. The doctor assured the anxious parents that there was nothing to worry about, but they would have to keep the baby in until the temperature went down.

SHAVEN-HEADED DANNY grabbed Kirk by his arms and pulled him forward. As Kirk's body jerked ahead, Danny thrust his knee full force into the boy's groin like a piston through an engine—one of those groin shots, so hard and so agonising that Kirk would feel the impact in years to come. Danny had learned that whenever he wanted to end a fight quickly, a knee to the groin was an accommodating weapon. It was a move taught to him by Teeko, one of the best black belts in the area. If you wanted to learn how to hurt the person trying to hurt you, Teeko was the guy to learn from. He especially taught his students how to fight dirty.

The fight drew a large number of boys after school to the 'usual spot', a short distance away. They came to cheer their two fourteen-year-old school mates on, as they battered the senses out of each other.

Urged on by his friends, Kirk somehow found the strength to lift himself up and, out of nowhere, threw a punch to Danny's jaw. Danny took it squarely, but it dazed him and he only just managed to respond with his own shot to the face. While Kirk shook his head to clear it, Danny pulled his opponent towards him by his Snoop Doggy Dogg plaits and followed his punch with another knee to the groin. Kirk was still fighting back. Danny put together a series of rights to the boy's head. With each punch, Kirk's head reeled back. But he took each blow like a man. Finally, Danny hit him so hard he felt his right hand crack. Kirk fell to the ground, blood pouring down his shirt. With his friends still urging him on, Kirk tried to raise his head, but couldn't. He tried again. He had to. He wasn't just fighting for himself, he was fighting for his crew, and as a scout for the Grange, he wasn't willing to let no Piper's boy triumph over him.

With blood dripping on his hooded sweatshirt, Danny was led away by his friends, raising his arms in victory. When, further down the street, the full realisation of the beating sank in they got anxious and began running, as fast as their legs could carry them, dodging cars and pedestrians to make it back to their area. When they got there Danny raced through the entrance to his estate. At last he was home.

THEY DROVE IN silence. Jigsy's mood was deep, dark and raging, his eyes on fire. Teeko, beside him at the wheel of his Jeep, had watched him chasing the angry dragon all day. And now he looked run down and tired. Teeko had mentioned it already, that the shit was making him paranoid, but Jigsy became angry and accused Teeko of running scared. Now he was searching frantically in the glove compartment.

"You already smoked it," Teeko said in anticipation.

"I don't fucking remember having no smoke," Jigsy said angrily.

"You dig, Jigs. That shit is drying up your brain

cells."

"Just drive, man," Jigsy said.

The Jeep cruised ahead, Teeko not too happy with the crack head business, but his mind temporarily distracted by a particularly attractive young lady on the other side of the road, dressed to kill and looking over in his direction. Jigsy didn't even notice her. He was thinking of the things he needed to sort out as a matter of urgency. A pipe, he decided, would have a better effect on his thinking, instead of having to make roll ups all the time. He resolved to get one as soon as possible.

Teeko slowed down to a crawl, smiling across to the girl, who smiled back, when Jigsy unexpectedly asked, in a low voice:

"Teeko, what do you think we should do about this situation?"

"Me? You asking me?" Teeko had already made his views known. "I told you before. Confrontation and eradication. But first..." He looked down at Jigsy's shaky hand, "you've got to be able to shoot straight."

IT WAS LATE night. With very little money on him, Zukie made his way down to the Cowesby Street blues looking for Chico. He crossed over to the other side of Broadfield Road and ducked into an alley. A wet chill tickled the back of his neck.

At Cowesby Street, he surveyed the row of parked cars, BMW's, Golfs, Astras, Sierras, Escorts, and a Jag, all looking out of place against the dirty, dilapidated abandoned houses at the end of the street.

The sound of thumping bass was clearly audible. Zukie hoped that Chico was still here.

The steel, reinforced front door opened outwards. As it did, a burst of loud music drifted out along with a general atmosphere of laughter and heat.

Inside the smoky blues, Zukie made his way towards the kitchen-cum-bar. He had to get rid of his coat.

"Yaaaow! Bann-I!" Zukie shouted to a dark-skinned dread behind the counter of the makeshift bar. "W'happen dread? Tek dis one fe me nuh, star?"

Still nodding his head in time to the beat, with eyes

burning red, Bann-I took the army surplus camouflage jacket and placed it behind the counter.

"Bann-I," Zukie leant forward, "yuh seen Chico?"

"Who?" Bann-I asked, pouring a short.

Zukie leaned across again and shouted above the music. "Chico!"

Bann-I's face cleared for a moment and he nodded towards the main room. "Him in desso."

Zukie smiled with appreciation and disappeared into the darkness of the main dance room.

"Zukie!!"

A firm, strong hand gripped his shoulder and spun him around.

"Chico?" Zukie strained in the darkness to make out Chico's mane of unkempt dreadlocks.

"W'happen, rudebwai?" There was no mistaking his husky voice. "Where yuh been hiding, man? Me hear seh yuh fin' wuk."

Zukie shouted over the music. "Yeah, but it was only a few days work. It done already"

"What a bitch," Chico muttered. "So money tight again?"

Zukie nodded. Chico took his friend's hand and put a spliff in his palm. "Control dis, iya?"

Even though Zukie was crashing at Chico's mum's, Chico himself never seemed to be there. He always seemed to be out, "checkin' a daughter" or something. In the burst of light from a cigarette lighter, Zukie saw the gold sovereign rings on Chico's fingers and the heavy chain around his neck. Zukie wondered how Chico could have come across money to be able to buy jewellery. Concealing his surprise, he put the spliff to

141

his mouth and inhaled.

"Cum 'ere," Chico said in a strong Manchester accent, motioning Zukie out of the dark room. "Let's go out in the passage and rap a little."

In the passage, Chico nodded his acknowledgement to some guys by the bar. Zukie didn't recognise them.

"Bann-I," Chico shouted, "get me a Special. Zukie, what yuh having?"

Zukie shrugged his shoulders. "Get me a Dragon."

They took their drinks and made their way to a corner where they could talk a bit easier.

"So you win the lottery since me see you las', or is the sound business doing good?" Zukie asked.

Chico laughed. "Sound business nah mek no money," he replied. One of the men by the bar was beckoning him over. "Soon come," he told Zukie.

Zukie pulled heavily on Chico's spliff. His eyes locked into the men. One of them was tall with funki-dreds, his face serious. The other was half a head shorter and had wild, bloodshot eyes. He smiled at Zukie through narrow eyes.

"Who are they?" asked Zukie when Chico returned.

"Friends, good people, y'know. They thought you reminded them of someone," Chico said casually, shrugging his shoulders. "No big t'ing."

Zukie coughed as the smoke from the spliff stalled in his throat. This was good sensi, not the regular bush weed.

"Spliff getting to you?" Chico laughed.

They stood and took in the atmosphere for a moment. The session was filling up. It was obviously the place to be tonight. Even Hair Oil was there, freckles dancing around his smiling face, with a bottle of stout in one hand and a paper cup in the other, and with the baby dreadlocks he previously had totally gone. A smooth, neat, close-to-the-scalp cut replaced it.

"W'happen, rudebwai?" Zukie said laughing. "Me never recognise yuh fe true. What we gwine call you now, 'Crazy Baldhead'?" Zukie's eyes dropped down to the gold chains hanging over a brand new silk shirt. "Better mind man nuh tax unuh fe yuh chains an' t'ing."

Chico and Hair Oil roared with laughter.

"Come on, let's celebrate."

"What's there to celebrate, Chico?"

"Big t'ings ah gwan, man!!"

SNAPPER AND FRENCHIE were off their guard when they stepped into the party. It was all the way out in Whalley Range, and they weren't expecting any trouble. They were just there to look for girls — somebody said that the party was going to have "two criss gal fe every man!" — and to distribute leaflets advertising a birthday dance they were keeping.

Slim's huge bulk occupied a corner of the main room, when they came in. It was dark and they appeared not to have seen him. He saw the two youths in leather jackets enter and go into the crowded, dimly-lit main room of the party. The tall one with the baseball cap was skinny, the other one was short and fat, had jheri curls and wore several earrings in one ear. When he got a good look at them he didn't recognise them as Grange, but when he saw the leaflets they were distributing, he knew they were. Nobody else but Grange would have a dance at the Carib, especially after the recent hit. He was incensed that the Grange would dare to come out here to his cousin's yard, to her party!

Frenchie went to the next room to check the food runnings. Snapper said he'd see him there in a moment. First, he was going to check a particularly fly girl who was dancing by herself, seductively, next to one of the speakers. He moved over to her with a broad smile.

There was no central light in the room, only a small light where the sound was, but Slim could make out Snapper alright and he didn't like the fact that the Grange bwai was moving in on his sister. He crossed the floor, shoving aside the ravers dancing to the 'slow jam' tune.

Snapper saw the man pushing his way towards him. He didn't know him, but realised there was going to be trouble. The larger youth barged into his shoulder, very obviously and deliberately with a lot of bulk behind him. It was no accident.

It was dark in the room and the fighting was all over in a matter of seconds. The Grange boy pushed Slim who pushed him back. The two fat youths were pushing each other and swearing. Then they started hitting each other. They threw blows, fast and furious at each other, and the needle on the sound system's turntable began jumping and the music hopping. Slim was punching so fast and hard, Snapper didn't know what was happening.

When the lights finally came on, Snapper had been stabbed. He staggered out the room holding his stomach with both hands. Frenchie didn't have time to consider the shock of seeing his friend with blood seeping through his fingers, but grabbed him and helped him as best he could quickly out into the car.

OUTMANNED AND OUTGUNNED, Storm crashed through the window in the Old Lady's living room. Out on the street he sprinted in the direction of the railway line. Gripping his gun he ran like a hunted man, with police sirens screaming all around him...

He awoke from the nightmare crumpled up in the corner of his bedroom, his legs pulled tightly to his chest. He wept until he could cry no more, and then lay on his back wondering what was next.

Storm heard the voice calling him, but couldn't be sure if it was real or part of the dream. His whole body felt numb and too heavy to move. The voice continued to call him forward to come and pay his last respects, at his own funeral.

Storm shook himself quickly, panicking, cold sweat trickling down his forehead. It took him a few minutes to make out what day it was, and to remember all the bad news given to him during the many mobile conversations with Lewty.

He tried to calm himself down, tried to still his heart beating madly in his chest. He was glad to be alive.

THE GOLF GTi swerved quickly onto the forecourt of the petrol station on Great Western Street. It was late evening and the place was unusually deserted for that time of night. But taking into account recent events, this didn't surprise Jigsy. It made things easier for what they were about to do. The less people about the better.

Jigsy touched a switch and the electric window on the passenger side slid down.

"I don't feel too good about this!!" Bluebwai said, suddenly very nervous.

At the wheel, Easy-Love turned towards the back seat, looking over his dark round shades.

"So wha', yuh scared of a bit of fireworks?"

Bluebwai shifted uneasily on his seat and pulled his baseball cap firmly over his red and sweaty face.

"No fucking way, Easy!"

Bluebwai had been on edge ever since Fluxy got hit. He wanted to get the Grange as much as anybody else, pay them back for what they did to Fluxy, but since the shooting, Piper Mill had lacked any serious leadership and all they were doing was looking for trouble. Jigsy had assumed his brother's position without authority. And instead of trying to pull the crew together at this time of crisis, Jigsy listened to Easy-Love, who's attitude had become renk in the last few days.

The atmosphere in the car was tense for a long moment. Easy-Love lit a cigarette and gave Blue one which seemed to ease the tension. He then climbed out of the car to fill the tank, cigarette still in hand. Blue was still uneasy, but for the moment his mind got back to the purpose of their being at the petrol station. He wasn't in favour of hitting the Grange this way, but he was just a youth, and had no choice but to go along when Jigsy insisted. Every Piper man had been itching for a scrap with the Grange since their leader fell. Blue had to just go with the flow. So they had got a set of hot wheels for the runnings they had to do tonight.

It hadn't escaped Jigsy's notice that Storm had kept a low profile since Fluxy's killing. His flat in Moss Side, on the estate near Grange Close, had been empty for days and no one had seen his BMW anywhere. To the Pipers, his disappearance was as good as a confession of guilt. They would have to smoke him out, wherever he was. It hadn't taken long for Jigsy to get the information he needed. He had decided to start hitting the Grange where they would feel it, where Storm would feel it, in the heart of his operation. He wanted Storm for himself, but he intended to deliver up the entire Grange operation to the Pipers. He had sent word out to his scouts to get him information on the Grange dealers, where they were operating from and when. This petrol station was one of the Grange's most successful outlets. All night long youths would amble by and thrust a note into the silver tray in the window, and the attendant would shove a tiny parcel into the tray back to them. But at the moment, things were quiet.

"This one is easy," Jigsy said casually, as Easy-Love climbed back into the car. He was studying the young, blond-haired attendant in the petrol station shop. "Okay, let's do it."

From the look on his face, Bluebwai still wasn't sure about this one. He felt anxious, a little bit afraid and wanted to get the hell away.

It was as if Jigsy could feel his vibes. He looked at the

youngster and smiled confidently.

"Yout'man, settle," Jigsy reassured. He reached in the back seat, on the floor next to Blue, and pulled up a pump-action shotgun. It took Jigsy only a moment to snap the gun into place and then he stepped out of the car, leisurely, the hood of his sweatshirt pulled low over the bandanna around his head, a scarf around his face, and the shotgun hidden under his trench coat. "Come soon!" he called out back to his friends in the car. It was an old joke of Jigsy to always say "come soon" instead of "soon come."

Clive James was on TV, grinning like a fat Cheshire cat. The station attendant glanced up as the black youth walked towards him. He became immediately suspicious because the guy was wearing a scarf over his face, but his brain was too slow in making a decision for him. The black youth already stood before him, on the other side of the glass. He looked briefly at the youth and searched his eyes for any sign of recognition, but there was none. His eyes were about the only thing he could see, and for a moment he wondered why the youth was dressed so oddly.

"That'll be £10.00, please," the attendant said.

With a gloved hand Jigsy placed a crumpled ten pound note into the metal cash tray for the petrol.

"Was there anything else?" the attendant asked quizzically, staring deep into the black youth's red eyes.

"Yeah, there was something else," Jigsy answered. He looked up casually. "Twenty Benson and Hedges, a kingsize Rizla... And..." Jigsy held the attendant in a cold, deadly stare, before continuing slowly, "one more t'ing..." He paused. "Is this glass shotgun proof?"

148

THE WALLS GLARED silently back at Storm. He felt uneasy. Jasmine should have returned home with Lee ages ago. Supposing something had happened to them? No, impossible. Nobody knew who they were or where they lived. Besides Withington was a little distance from where it was all happening, and he could cool out here without worrying about being hounded by anybody. Storm always kept his tracks covered, to protect his family.

Moss Side was still crawling with police following the shooting at the Shabba concert. Cops seemed to be everywhere, even in the skies, where helicopters hovered above the streets. But it wouldn't last long, Storm thought. Things would cool off and the gangs would go underground for a while. Just for a while. But the war was still on. This thing wasn't over until it was over.

The sound of the front door slamming shook Storm out of his deep thoughts. Jasmine walked into the living room, her twists tied back in a ponytail and holding a late edition copy of the Manchester Evening News. Lee followed her in and ran straight to his father.

"What's happening, rudebwai? How was nursery today?" he asked, ruffling the child's hair. "Jazzy, where you been so long?"

Jasmine simply stared at Storm through her oversize spectacles with a look of pain. He felt her eyes boring through to his soul.

"Worried, were you?" She didn't expect him to admit it. "I was walking in the park. I took the long way. I needed to think."

"About what?" he said, only half-interested.

She glared down at him, seated comfortably on the sofa in front of the TV, wondering how he could just go on pretending. Then she held up the newspaper and shoved the front page in front of him.

Storm read the headline: 'GANG WAR'. He didn't need to read the rest and he knew what she was getting at, he got the general picture. He cast her a deep-set, wary stare. All he could do was kick back and watch the ride. He hung his head, bit his lip. Sighing and looking back up at her, he said, "Just cool nuh, Jazz."

This time she wasn't going to be cool. She told Lee to go to his room and draw. The little boy did as he was told, reluctantly. Jasmine was angry, but maintained her voice at a low level.

"You really don't know what's happening, do you Cliff?" she asked. It hurt to know that nothing had changed between them, that he was still prepared to live this dangerous, mad life. He was still determined to stay on the road that led to destruction. Like all the others, one by one, they were heading for the cemetery. She

150

fought back the tears. "No, you really don't. All this killing... Who do you think's really winning, Cliff? And who do you think the losers are? You ever hear of the endangered species, Cliff?"

Fuming, Cliff jumped up, shouting at her, "I don't need all this hassling from you! What makes you think I've got anything to do with any gang war?"

She took a long hard look at him before answering slowly and directly.

"Because you always do, Cliff."

IN THE BACKGROUND, tough ragamuffin gun lyrics buzzed gently through the sophisticated four-way speaker systems:

After seven o'clock me shoot anyt'ing wha' move,
Fifty shot me fire, fifty man dead,
Thirty full of copper, twenty full ah lead.

"What's the next move?" Jigsy asked, his red eyes darting around in his head frantically. He was pacing up and down in his small, neat apartment, punching his right fist into his left palm as he walked.

Easy sat in the armchair watching him. He was becoming irritated. He glanced over at the framed picture of Fluxy and Jigsy on the bookshelf, arms wrapped around each other, taken only a few months ago. "Flush him out," he replied.

Jigsy stopped in his tracks and looked incredulously

at Easy. "In't that what we're doin'?!" he screamed.

Easy looked up at him casually, then back at the small revolver resting in his hand. "No, we're trying to smoke him out and he in't comin'." He cleared his throat and looked directly at Jigsy, holding him in a steady gaze. "It's a different thing altogether. We've been trying to smoke him out and he in't coming, so we've got to flush him out."

"What the fuck is the difference?"

Easy had to stop himself rolling his eyes upwards. Fluxy would know. Easy kept his voice calm. He leaned forward, trying to spell it out for Jigsy.

"If he in't coming out, we're going to have to pick up some of his boys and make them talk."

"What about the raids?"

"We'll carry on with the raids, but if that shithead won't show himself, we got to capture some of his boys. The main ones, like Lewty. That's the only way."

Jigsy was unsure of whether that was the best move. He started to contemplate.

Easy kissed through his teeth.

"Suit yourself, you're the boss! If it was down to me, I'd have Storm out long, long time."

Jigsy looked at him angrily, offended that Easy thought he could do a much better job. Maybe he was right, but Jigsy didn't think so.

"How the fuck are you going to do that?"

"I'm just waiting for you to give me the go ahead," Easy said. "Me sick of all this skylarking. What we waiting for? You asked me what I should do, I told you. Time come now."

Jigsy looked down at the photo of himself and Fluxy.

He picked it up and wiped some dust of it with the sleeve of his jumper. "Okay," he said finally. "Okay, we'll do like you said."

Easy-Love smiled.

T EPID WATER FLOWED over his body. He welcomed the soothing feeling, but the water couldn't wash his thoughts away. The shower temporarily refreshed him, revitalising his tired senses. Eyes closed, Clifton reached blindly for the soap which slipped through his wet grasp. He cursed angrily. Bending down, he opened his eyes against the flow of the water. Suddenly, he was aware of a presence behind the shower curtain.

Storm feigned a whistle, reaching down for the hand gun, fully loaded, on the shower ledge. With a wild, violent thrust he wrenched the floral shower curtain back, pointing his gun right between the eyes.

Jasmine screamed at the sight of the gun.

"Cliff, it's only me!"

He relaxed instantly.

"Jazzy, I'm sorry. You sneaked up on me." He smiled at her reassuringly. She had definitely changed her image, he was thinking. It was subtle, but she was now more feminine compared to when they first started going out with each other.

With the threat over, Jazzy breathed more easily, but her tone remained angry.

"Get that thing out of my face!! I want it out of the house!!"

"Settle yuhself. The gun's safe," he said, pushing the safety catch.

"I don't want it in my house!"

"What do you want me to do? Walk out with it, naked?"

He stepped out of the shower quickly, examining his face only briefly in the cabinet mirror. His hair was already growing out and the sharp parting in it had almost disappeared. He wrapped a towel around himself.

"Don't ignore me, Cliff. That shooting the other night has got something to do with you, hasn't it?"

Clifton turned to look at her, the briefest hint of a smile on his lips, his jaw clenched tight and his cleft chin protruding..

"It's written all over your face," she continued. "It's never going to stop, is it?"

Clifton looked at her, expressionless. He didn't know what the answer to that was, he truly didn't. He wanted it to stop, but his crew were getting dissed all over the place, and he had to do something.

"I can't just stand by and let them walk all over us," he muttered to himself. "Nobody's going to walk over us."

"Very soon, Cliff," she said slowly, painfully, "there'll be no one left to walk over. Nobody. No Cheetham Panthers, no Pipers, no Grange, no Dodds. Nothing. All the black youth of Manchester will be rotting in graves or prison. What about Lee? Him next? You wanna see him follow in your footsteps?"

Clifton swallowed, a sour look on his face. He stared at her.

"I'm going out," she said, tears forcing their way through. She pushed past him. "When I come back, I don't want to see you or that gun here."

"CLIFF?" THE VOICE asked.

"Lalah, it's me."

Storm was calling the hospital from a phonebox not far from Jasmine's house. It took them a long while to connect the call through to the private room he had recently paid to have Lalah and the baby moved to.

"Where are you? I need you. Where are you?" Her voice was about to break. "I keep phoning your mobile and it's switched off all the time. Is everything okay?"

"Never mind me. Things level," he said dismissively, and asked how she and the baby were doing.

"The baby's fine and I'm okay. We should be out soon. I've decided on a name for her... Tia. It means 'the dawn'."

Storm said the name was beautiful for a beautiful daughter. Dawn, the beginning of a new day. That's what he needed in his life. Tia was part of his new dawn. A major part of it.

ST. MARY'S HOSPITAL is situated close to Manchester Royal Infirmary. Pam had been at the hospital every day, waiting and praying her boyfriend would pull through. He was still in a serious condition, but it was no longer critical.

Pam was Rough's girlfriend, and when she first saw him in intensive care after his beating, she was afraid. Afraid that he wouldn't make it, afraid that at the age of sixteen she was going to become a 'widow'. Fortunately, his condition became stable.

There wasn't much else to do. She was either at the hospital, or she was sitting around in his flat with her fingers crossed. The joy had gone out of her life with the attack on her boyfriend. She no longer went raving with her friends, she no longer cared to dress stylish and she didn't even bother wearing make-up anymore. Rough hadn't said anything to the police, but he had told her (he had to, she was his woman) who his assailants were, who had beaten him up so bad. Her heart, her soul, every joint of her body was aching with hate for them. Rough hadn't done anything to deserve it.

It was while cleaning the flat that she found it, behind the fridge, a heavy-looking revolver. She almost leapt out of her skin as she picked it up, caressing the cold metal nervously.

Immediately, she took the gun and wrapped it in a plastic carrier bag, her hands shaking all the while. Still carrying the revolver, she stood leaning on the kitchen work top, trying to stop her heart bursting through her chest. Although the Pipers were responsible for the attack on Rough, she knew that the baldheaded one, Teeko Martial, was the main assailant. She knew he drove a jeep. A red Suzuki jeep.

Had Rough Cut known what Pam was planning to do, he would have stopped her. Despite her young years she was a good woman, and he couldn't afford to lose her. She was a virgin when they first met. Just fifteen and chaste. And she denied him that territory for a long time. Until her sixteenth birthday, by which time they'd been together a year, and knew how much they both cared for each other. It had been the ultimate pleasure, pure and sweet ecstasy. Their relationship grew even more after that. She was like his younger sister, his mother, his best friend. Sometimes, they would stay in bed for a week, just letting each other know how much they meant to each other. He couldn't afford to lose her, not for nobody.

THE STREET WAS dark. He was at the top of Yarburgh Street, near the junction of Withington Road which leads into the area of Whalley Range. Teeko pulled up outside his woman's place. Late night. He couldn't remember when he last ate, but he was 'dead fe hungry' now. He paused in the Jeep to light a spliff. Winding down the window he tossed the used match out. Before he could wind the window back up, a gun was in his ear. A voice told him to move slowly out of the car. Holding his hands up in surrender, silently cursing, he dropped the burning spliff and did what he was ordered to do. But he wasn't going to let nobody shoot him without a fight. He had barely stepped out of the Jeep when his leg came flying out in a 'roundhouse' kick to the head of his assailant, who was sent flying to the ground. He heard a shot go off, felt it whizz by his ear as he dived to the ground instinctively. The second blast exploded as he crash-landed to the ground. He managed to roll under the Jeep for cover. Two more shots. His heart pumped like a piston, his mind raced with fear, then anger as he tried to roll out the other side, holding his head down with his hands. Flat on the ground, all alone, he felt a sick despair in the pit of his stomach. He thought about his mother and father and his two young children, and the insanity of the life he was living. This was the very reason the mothers of his children kept his kids away from him. It's a good thing this fucker don't know how to shoot straight, he thought to himself, by way of relief. He listened. There was silence. He looked up cautiously from under the Jeep. Saw the gunman squeezing the trigger in vain. The gun had jammed. Quickly, before the gunman could make a run for it, Teeko rolled out from under the Jeep.

The gunman was already off, down the road. His would-be assassin was no match for Teeko, and he quickly caught up with him.

He threw the punches, hard and direct, straight to the face. The gunman dropped the gun, the hood fell off. It was then that Teeko realised it was a girl disguised as a boy.

Teeko's momentary surprise was all the girl needed. She suddenly kicked him viciously and squarely in his testicles. He was doubled over in agony, grunting, holding his groin, his eyes watering.

The girl didn't hang around, but raced down the road

as fast as she could. Teeko called after her.

"Bitch! Next time I won't pussy around!"

He swore loudly but, at the sound of police sirens coming his way, limped quickly to his Jeep, breathing heavily. The girl disappeared into the vastness of the Alexandra Park Estate. It would be almost impossible to find her now. Teeko was still recovering from the surprise attack as he drove off. He was too angry to remember his hunger and that he came to visit his woman. He definitely wasn't expecting an ambush from a gangsta bitch. He wondered what Bruce Lee would have done in his position.

160

STORM DROVE HIS son out of town, to Oldham, where nobody would recognise them. All the way they chatted, father to son. Storm asked his son about how he liked his nursery school, and teased him about being popular with the girls. They drove to a park where they spent most of the morning together. It was a chance to spend quality time with a son who eagerly anticipated and needed his father's attention. Storm remembered how he had never had the chance to play with his father, or to do sports at school with his father encouraging his every move from the sidelines. He looked across to Lee who was playing on the slide. He seemed contented, laughing. A man walked a dog close by and smiled at them. The day was windy, but free of rain. Storm looked at his watch. He would have liked to be with Lee some more, but it was after one and he didn't want to keep his mobile switched off too long.

When he called Lee over, his son suspected it was time to go. Storm saw a dejected look in his son's eyes.

"You're not going to stay and play with me, Daddy?"

Lee asked. Storm shook his head miserably. How could he explain to Lee that he had other commitments, to the friends in his crew. He was sure that even his four-year-old son would have picked that up as a lame excuse. He was neglecting Lee and that was all there was to it.

Lee felt crushed. Storm promised that he would make it up to him. He sighed. The pressures of the bad bwai life were wearing him down mentally and physically. But like a roller-coaster ride that was getting faster, there was no way out.

IT WAS FAIRLY common knowledge on the streets that Jigsy and the others were going around threatening to deal with any Grange person they came across. It was difficult to go anywhere in Moss Side without stumbling on a heated altercation between gang members. Youths got hit over the head with bottles and, on more than one occasion, abandoned their girlfriends at parties where they were pursued by rival gang members. No one was prepared to attack in situations where they were outnumbered.

Several times members of the Pipers made forays into Grange territory in search of someone to fight, threatening anyone they came across, but if they were outnumbered they always backed off to return. Storm heard all about it on his mobile. He heard about how a couple of Pipers carrying a zip-up holdall, containing a double-barrelled shotgun, entered the youth club on the estate and fired both barrels in the ceiling, shouting,

"Grange bwai... you can hide but you can't run. We'll find you wherever you are!" Fortunately, no Grange people were there at the time, otherwise blood would have definitely spilled. He heard also about the fist fights and the stabbings, and he heard the chilling threats. He heard about how Sly, who had only just come out of the youth detention centre the other day, was threatened outside his home with a gun, made to get into a car and driven to the Piper Mill pub to see if anyone there recognised him as being a Grange man. Fortunately for Sly, nobody recognised him and they let him go.

Storm wanted to get his own back. He had been publicly humiliated. He was unable to defuse the situation and now everybody expected him to deal with the Pipers severely and soon. It was principally the heavy police presence on the streets which dissuaded him from making his move immediately. Jigsy was a hardcore bad bwai and crazy enough to not give a fuck, but Storm wanted out of this lifestyle. The payback was going to drop when things cooled off, but for now it was best he stayed out of sight. The last thing he needed was the police on his case too.

ZUKIE HEARD THE Old Lady call as he entered. He ignored her call and just climbed the stairs, two by two, up to his room. It wasn't the first time he had been back home since his mother threw him out. He had been by a few days earlier to collect his giro. And he was only coming back now to accompany his mother and brother to Vermont's funeral, the father he never knew. He needed to get the black jeans in his bedroom, a white shirt and a black blazer.

It was when he returned to collect his dole cheque, that Cliff told him about their dad dying the day before. At first, Zukie didn't know what he meant. He really didn't. For him, his father had never existed. And it was out of no sense of duty that he decided to attend the funeral, but from a sense of curiosity. Zukie wanted to pick up any bits of information about this man who had never existed, yet without whom *he* would never have existed.

Up in his room, Zukie heard Cliff calling him, but he decided to ignore him. Shortly after, Storm came bursting in the room enraged.

"Why the hell won't you answer when I'm calling you, when the Old Lady's calling you? Hmnnh? What's the matter with you?"

Zukie raised his hand as if to dismiss his brother. By now the Old Lady had joined them, standing in the doorway just behind her elder son. Zukie looked up and sighed. His room suddenly got too crowded. Without acknowledging either his mother or his brother, he brushed past them through the door, heading back downstairs. Clifton watched him for a moment stunned, then shouted his brother's name and, at the same time, ran after him, catching him on the landing. Clifton's anger took hold of him and he tackled his brother from behind, knocking him down the stairs. Zukie managed to pull Cliff down with him, and the Old Lady screamed for the Lord and reached for the inhaler in her pocket as she caught sight of her two sons rolling down the stairs. At the bottom, the struggle continued. The two brothers fought each other rolling, wrestling, grappling, fists flying wildly, armlocking, bending fingers, squeezing throats and cursing each other. Zukie may have had the technique, but Storm was more muscular and had more stamina. He finally held his younger brother in a grip that restrained him. The Old Lady looked at Clifton appealingly, silent eyes tearful and pleading. Clifton reassured her that he wasn't even hurting Zukie.

"You can't touch me!" Zukie cried breathlessly.

"I just want to talk to you like a brother, that's all. If something's wrong, maybe I can help you!"

"You can stay out of my life, that's how you can help me," Zukie shouted back. He continued to struggle as best he could, kicking his legs out. Storm forced him face down on to the carpet, holding him down with the weight of his body, and twisting his arm behind his back.

"If I get up, I'll fucking kill you," Zukie snarled.

"It's okay, Mum," Clifton assured again. " It's cool. I'll have it sorted. Zukie, I understand how you feel."

"Now you understand how I feel!" Zukie exclaimed, his voice shrieking with disbelief. "That's right, tell me that you know how I feel to ease your fucking conscience. You think you can buy people. Like the Old Lady. Buying all that furniture and stuff... Why don't you tell her Cliff, why don't you tell her how you really make your money, Cliff? Why don't you tell her that you're a gangbanger, and how the whole town thinks that you killed Fluxy."

Now Clifton was angry, but it was too late. The Old

Lady came down from upstairs and confronted Clifton.

"Did you?" Her question was blunt and precise. "Did you kill somebody?"

"No!" Clifton responded. He let Zukie get up. "I wasn't even in Manchester when he got shot!"

That was all the Old Lady needed to hear. She wasn't interested in rumours. If Clifton said he wasn't anything to do with it, she believed him. End of story.

Zukie uttered a laugh of disbelief. With desperation and anguish in his voice, Clifton addressed his brother:

"I tell you before I never kill him. You just won't listen. If I wanted to dust Fluxy I had plenty of opportunities. But there was no need."

Zukie could hear the trembling in his brother's voice.

"What if the cops hear the gossip?" Zukie asked

"It don't matter to me, 'cause I'm innocent. Kill Fluxy? Chuh, you ought to know me, man. I'm your own brother."

"No, no I don't know you. I don't know anything about you at all."

"You don't, unh? Well listen up, I was the one who looked after you when we were kids. When you was in trouble I was there to help, to take care of you. Always."

"But that was then," Zukie retorted. "I knew you then. I don't know you now," he said, drawing in a deep breath and shaking his head slowly, regretfully.

"Well I'm still here to take care of you," Storm said after a long pause, looking at Zukie seriously, "if you need me."

"Is that supposed to make me feel good?" Zukie asked.

Storm hung his head.

166

"Why don't you give it up?" Zukie continued. "Is it all worth the death threats? Are you able to sleep at nights? Why don't you just get out of it and stay out of their way?"

Storm didn't want to answer. He knew he could get up and walk away, but what about Lewty, what about Rough, Colours? What about the crew? They wouldn't turn their backs on him if he needed them.

"Zukie, I know you hate me. And I know things in't ever going to be the same between us, like it used to be. But you're my brother. All I know is I care for you."

For all his sincerity, Clifton's words made little impact on his brother. Zukie felt that caring for each other meant more than just uttering the words. If Clifton cared enough about his family, he would be concerned about the way drugs were affecting their neighbourhood. Zukie considered Clifton too selfish to really care about anyone but himself.

Clifton didn't bother to continue arguing. He was exhausted. Besides, time was running out. If they didn't make a move quickly, they would be late for the funeral.

ZUKIE STOOD WITH one arm folded across his chest, the other under his chin, his head tilted, a frown on his face, his hair tied into a sandy ponytail, wondering what he was doing there. His spirit wasn't inside him in the huge church. His eyes were fixed on the open coffin by the altar and he was thinking it was funny how things turn out. Life was a strange road to travel. There were no clues as to how long the journey would last, so you needed to do your thing and make your peace while you could. Vermont never knew his life would come to an end so soon, or that the son he had never known would be at his funeral, staring down on his lifeless face, with no emotion. For Zukie felt no feeling of loss. On the contrary, he felt that it was Vermont who had lost out on the opportunity of knowing his sons. It was his loss. Life never gives you a second chance to rectify your mistakes. The congregation sang a mournful hymn. Funerals were morbid affairs, Zukie thought.

It was no surprise to his family that Vermont's eldest children, Grace, Phillip and Neville did not attend their father's funeral. Grace in Canada declined the invitation, while Phillip and Neville in the United States both said they were otherwise engaged. The funeral of a father they had not seen for a quarter of a century was far from uppermost in their minds. The Old Lady stuck out like a 'black girl in the ring (tra-la-la-la-la)'. Hers was the darkest face in the church. The majority of the faces were very light-skinned or white like Imelda, representing Vermont's and his wife's families, respectively. The Old Lady's own son Zukie, paled next to her. Even Clifton, whose complexion was closest to hers, was a shade or two lighter. But that didn't bother her. If anything, it made her even more proud. She could hold her own next to the best of the Michaels.

The sudden chill in the church when the priest declared to the congregation that Vermont had been a "good father," felt to Zukie like the spirits of a thousand restless duppies, lost, haunting souls, stirred from their slumber. Zukie stretched his legs. Cliff, flanking the Old Lady on the other side, glanced at his watch, stifled a yawn and looked pissed off that his father's funeral was taking up so much of his time.

They were positioned in the pew just behind the main family. Zukie looked at the backs of his step-family's head and wondered what was occupying their thoughts. For some reason his half-brother, Vermont's son, Eugene, kept glancing back and staring at Clifton. It was a strange look that Zukie couldn't quite interpret.

One by one they filed past the open coffin. Some peered in, whispering. Some chose to hurry past. Vermont's second wife paused at the silk-lined casket, weeping and crying hysterically.

Zukie looked down at the body. He didn't want to admit that he in any way resembled the lifeless face in the coffin, but he couldn't deny it. Despite the grey hairs and the bald patch, despite the wrinkles, this was his father, there was no doubt about it.

The Old Lady looked down at Vermont for the briefest of moments, refusing to allow the aged and embalmed image of him in the coffin to be her lasting impression of him. Then, with her eyes closed, she whispered to her husband's spirit:

"I bring dem, Monty. You wanted to see dem. I bring dem. I shoulda bring dem before you pass away, but my heart was hard. I'm sorry."

Zukie and Cliff exchanged confused looks. Zukie turned to her. She was calm, dignified, seemingly at peace with herself. To Zukie's surprise, she held his hand in hers. As they filed past the coffin, Clifton placed a supportive hand on his brother's shoulder.

169

"YOU HAVE A light?" Storm asked Eugene, as he stepped out of the church hall, where many of Vermont's friends were gathered with his family for drinks and to exchange memories of the dearly departed.

Eugene eyed him suspiciously for a moment, before swaggering over to his new-found half-brother, a cheap lighter in his hand. He knew who Storm was. Storm lit his cigarette and thanked him, looking the boy up and down, baggy black jeans and the black bomber jacket.

It was the first good look at his half-brother, and now Storm could see what several of the other mourners were already aware of, that Zukie and Eugene looked so much alike they were like full-blooded brothers, both favouring their father. He thought he recognised something else about Eugene also. Storm inhaled the smoke, keeping his eyes on the boy.

Eugene was cool, unaffected, giving nothing away. Storm said he knew he must be feeling bad. Eugene simply shrugged his shoulders.

"How long you known you had half-brothers?" Storm continued, pulling deeply on the cigarette. The voices from the reception behind them were rising as someone was recounting a particularly interesting story about Vermont, to the appreciation of everyone else present. To Storm, it was more important to know his brother than to remember his father.

Eugene cleared his throat and swallowed nervously.

170

He passed his hand over his mouth. Storm thought he noticed the hand trembling slightly. "I found out this morning, an hour before the service... My dad never once told me..."

Eugene looked as if he was having a hard time adjusting to the reality of the situation.

"Do you have a problem with it?"

Eugene fixed Storm an inquisitive, blue-eyed stare. "Maybe... maybe not," he said. "Depends."

"On what?" Storm asked, curious.

"Dunno..." the younger boy replied, with a shrug of his shoulders.

"It is different," Storm said, "because we're blood, Eugene. It's gotta make a difference. You are my brother and I am my brother's keeper," Storm said. "Anyone touch you, dem touch me too, seen?"

He held up his clenched fist for Eugene to punch. After an indecisive moment, Eugene pulled his right hand out of his bomber jacket and touched his brother's fist lightly.

THE MAN THEY were looking for was smart, covering his tracks. He stepped out of a car they didn't recognise as his. They were looking for a 'G' registration Volkswagen. It was only through a stroke of luck that they recognised him when he pulled up at the traffic lights next to them, in a new registration, silver Carlton, wearing the same grey Trilby he had worn in court. They ran a check on the car and discovered that it had been hired using a false name. They should have guessed. Like many of the villains in the area, Delroy Watkins made a habit of bouncing around and putting nothing in his name that would lead to his current address.

The two detectives looked at each other quizzically as the Carlton pulled up at the kerbside. They continued a bit further up the road in their unmarked vehicle before parking. From there, they watched the youth in their rearview mirror. He stepped out of the Carlton and walked hurriedly into the Sportsman Pub.

"So what d'you think he's doing in Old Trafford,

Barry?"

The young, dark-haired Detective Constable Barry Hodge, wearing a green bomber jacket shrugged his shoulders.

"Could be anything," he said. "Do you wanna check it or shall I?"

"You take it. I think he might have seen me at the traffic lights."

Barry nodded. He knew his job. He was to blend into the atmosphere of the Sportsman pub without people realising he was a policeman. He took a stick of chewing gum out of the packet on the dashboard and unwrapped it. Folding it in half, he inserted it into his mouth and started chewing. It was his lucky flavour. He paused, contemplating the course of action. "I'll go inside. You go round the back. Give it five minutes then come through, just in case."

The two men climbed out of their car and each went to play their respective part in the plot.

WHEN HE FINALLY looked at the car clock, Storm realised he had been driving for nearly two hours. The petrol gauge was on empty and so was he. Storm caught a glimpse of himself in his rear view mirror. Gaunt, tired, pale and bloodshot. He badly needed a shower. He also needed to eat.

Again, as soon as he switched off his mobile phone, he began to doubt that it was a good idea. He pulled up by the roadside, exhausted. If he could just rest for a minute, he would be able to think straight. He killed the engine and lit a cigarette. It left a bitter taste in his mouth. He needed to brush his teeth.

It felt so good to simply hit the road, going in no particular direction, with the gas pedal pushed all the way down to the floor and feel himself flying away from all his problems. Oh, if only it were that simple. He turned off the motorway to fill up with petrol and ended up in this sleepy, little town.

A thought crossed his mind. Wasn't it today that Lalah and Tia were due to be discharged from hospital? He flicked open his mobile phone. Shit! The 'Low Battery' sign was flashing. He looked around. A solitary delivery boy on a bicycle rode past him, stopped, got off his bike and leaned it up against a garden wall. Whistling happily, he carried a box of groceries into the open porch of a semi-detached house.

Storm lowered his window.

"Excuse me!" he called.

The blonde-haired, white boy eyed him suspiciously, hesitating as he weighed up the situation. He looked no older than fifteen. How innocent and unreal this place seems to be, Storm thought. Like one of those places you see on television advertisements where perfect families lived perfect lives.

"Yes?" The boy eventually answered.

"Where am I?"

"Montgomery Road." The boy answered, keeping a safe distance.

"What Town?"

"Coventry."

"Coventry?!" Storm repeated with disbelief.

174

The boy nodded nonchalantly.

"Where's the nearest phone box?"

"On the corner," the boy said, pointing to the end of the road and lifting the box of groceries along shouted, "See ya!" and carried on with his business.

THE SPORTSMAN COULD only be called a pub in the broadest of terms. Situated in Old Trafford, it was more like a restaurant and its customers, at this time of the day, were mostly people who came in for lunch. But it also had a well-stocked bar. The plainclothes officer took a seat a short distance away, not too close to arouse suspicion, but close enough to be able to eavesdrop. It wasn't easy, because the two black youths spoke in very low tones.

The detective sipped at his pint of beer and pulled out a pouch of tobacco, a red rizla and rolled one. He couldn't make a positive ID on the second black guy who was leaning over a bottle of stout, with his head hidden in the hood of the black leather jacket, but there was something vaguely familiar...

Out of the corner of his eye, he saw his man, agitated and in a gloomy mood. Something had upset him. The taller youth stayed cool, unperturbed, even expressing flashes of humour. They seemed to be discussing some business, but the detective could only catch bits and pieces:

"Raas claat...! Cool nuh rudebwai, settle the matter. Deal with it good. Today or tomorrow... You think it's cool to make a move now? There ain't no use for the both of us to get fucked up... Guns don't argue, seen?"

The two youths finally got up to leave. It was then that the police officer saw the butt of the revolver sticking out of the unidentified man's waistband. Shit, he thought. The fucker didn't seem to be too bothered who saw his piece. There was going to be trouble if either of them recognised him. If they thought he was on his own they would have no qualms about shooting him.

No serious drugs undercover officer could expect a threat-free career. Barry gladly suffered his enemies, because he wasn't in the police force to make friends. But he wasn't in it to be killed either. He weighed up his options for a moment. Shit. Where the fuck was Colin? He wished his partner was there with him. He sat still as they slowly made their way out, all the time watching both youths out of the corner of his eye for any signs of recklessness.

THE PICTURE WASN'T becoming any clearer to Storm. Something was missing. Something lacking, unclear, how it all came together so neatly that he should get the blame for Fluxy's death, the link to the chain of events which had hurtled him, in the last few weeks, to the position he was in now, feeling wrecked, miserable and tormented by guilt and frustration. So what was it? So how come all the suspicion fell on him so neatly, at a time when he had no alibi? And how come the rumour spread so fast, with even his own people coming up to him to ask him if he dusted Fluxy? It looked like a set-up. If so, what was it all about? And how far was it going to go? Somewhere in the back of his mind, an old tune was calling him:

> Walking down the road with a pistol in yuh waist
> Johnny you're too bad
> One of these days when you hear a voice say run
> Where yuh gonna run to?
> Yuh gonna run to the rocks for rescue, there will be no rock.

Storm was sitting in his attic bedroom under the roof of the Old Lady's house, thinking. The midi system behind his bed was tuned to Frontline Radio. Jack Radics' voice crooned over the airwaves. What are you going to do when it all goes wrong, Zukie had asked. Everything was going wrong now, and he still didn't have an answer. He wondered what Jigsy, convinced that he killed Fluxy, was planning next for him.

Storm picked up his pen shakily and, on a sheet of A4 paper, began to write a list of the unfolding events since Fluxy's death. Several sheets later, he paused to light a pre-rolled spliff, which had been lying on the bed. He inhaled slowly then returned to his list. Within these events was locked the name of the person who was really responsible. The Grange and Piper Mill wouldn't be trying to waste each other if Fluxy hadn't been killed. He would have been able to broker the peace which had been on his mind since he witnessed the birth of his daughter. Someone had set the two gangs at each other's throats on purpose. That someone was now somewhere, enjoying the pain and madness that had raged, gang against gang, man against man. That person was out there, somewhere, laughing at the fact that Storm couldn't sleep nor eat, and was forever looking behind him. So who killed Fluxy? Who dusted him? Who would profit most from a gang war between the Pipers and the Grange? Storm counted ten names on his list. He stared at the names long and hard, but was getting no closer to solving the mystery. He could draw up an endless list of names and still not get closer to finding who the deadly assassin was.

THE COPS HAD been watching outside in their unmarked vehicle, parked across the road from the house on Prenderghast Street, in Cheetham Hill. Barry was sitting in the car, eating McDonald's. Colin was round the back, it was his turn to eavesdrop. Anyway, Barry thought, as he took a bite of his quarter pounder with cheese, Colin understood the Jamaican dialect a lot better.

Because the living room blinds were slightly open at the back of the house, the detective was able to watch them making out on the settee. His suspect, Delroy Watkins, and his girlfriend, Pee-Wee. He watched them going at it excitely, she on top of him, lifting her hips up and sinking them down on top of him with ever greater rapidity, as she squeezed her breast sensually. He underneath, his Trilby cocked back, moaning and groaning and shouting, "Yes, oh yes, oh yes!"

The detective, a tall, athletic ebony-skinned Afro-Saxon with a confident smile and bold sideburns running down on either side of his face, was amazed that Bow-Bow was able to concentrate on sex after all the death threats he had been receiving. He watched as they changed position. Then Bow-Bow was on top of her, his head between her legs. The detective now understood how he had earned his nickname.

Detective Constable Colin Edwards also had a nickname. His colleagues at the nick insisted on calling him 'Chalky'. He inherited the name from the last black detective to have worked for the drugs squad. And the more he resented the name, the more his colleagues would use it. As his degree in Behavioural Psychology had taught him a leopard never changes its spots, he grudgingly accepted the nickname.

He couldn't help getting a hard-on himself as he watched Bow-Bow in action. His man was now pumping away at Pee-Wee from behind, doggy style. Edwards wondered whether Bow-Bow had ever read Freud's case study of the Wolf Man, whose psycho-pathological condition, Sigmund attributed to his having, as a baby, spied his father taking his mother from behind. Most probably Bow-Bow hadn't heard of the Wolf Man. Most probably he hadn't even heard of Sigmund Freud, the father of modern psychoanalysis. On top of everything else, Bow-Bow was a peasant.

Edwards continued watching as Bow-Bow carried on pumping into Pee-Wee from behind, she kneeling on the settee in front of him, her back to him, begging him not to stop. Bow-Bow did what he could, but it didn't last long. He came to his climax screaming blasphemously, his entire body jerking forward like the action of the hammer head on a power drill, causing his Trilby to fall off the back of his head. Still locked together, they both crashed on the settee, exhausted.

Suddenly Pee-Wee got nervous. "Shhh!" she said, listening. "I heard something." She pulled herself slightly from under him.

"The wind outside, branches," Bow-Bow said.

Pee-Wee was insistent. She rose up, pushing him off her completely. He landed on the floor. Edwards could hear the conversation clearly.

"There isn't a tree in the garden, yuh fool. Me seh me hear somet'ing."

Sighing, Bow-Bow slipped on his blue silk boxer shorts, as Pee-Wee covered her body with a pink silk robe.

"Relax, Pee, you're getting paranoid."

Pee-Wee glared at him. "You're used to living with bullets whistling past yuh earhole, I'm not."

Bow-Bow sighed, the passion having died for him. He picked up the small, silver-coloured pistol from on top of the television and went to investigate. He unbolted and unlocked the back door, sticking his neck out. Confident, he opened it wide. Smiling, he turned to Pee-Wee standing behind him.

"See, Pee-Wee, nothing there but the night."

Edwards let out his breath as the door closed from the inside. He had taken cover behind the shed, from where he could still hear Bow-Bow and Pee-Wee talking. To the detective, Bow sounded pussy-whipped and needed to sort out his woman.

"I think we should move from here, Delroy," she said.

180

"Way out. Like the country."

"How many dealers yuh see in the country, Pee?" Bow-Bow asked. "Look, we'll reason about it tomorrow. Let's get undressed again. I want you to talk to me dirty."

"You want dirty talk? See dirty talk yah. ME WAAN MOVE OUTTA DIS BLOODCLAAT, PUSSYCLAAT PLACE! Yuh understand now?"

"Jeeze, Pee-Wee!"

JASMINE SAT ON the sofa in her living room. Lee, wrapped around her legs, was asleep. She stroked his hair gently.

Clifton smiled and swallowed. They were staring at each other. Locked into each other's gaze, like they were studying each other closely for the first time. Looking at her, he was reminded of what had first attracted him to her. Those beautiful brown eyes.

"We'll buy a house. We'll move," he promised.

"How can you be so sure?" she asked.

He looked away, then back at her quickly. He felt close to her. She had wanted him close last night when she was feeling lonely.

"I'm as sure as I am standing here."

"So we're going to just pick up right where we left off?" she asked.

ZUKIE PAUSED. IT was the first time they had been alone together since the funeral. He returned home to pick up his music selection, including his Bob Marley classics and found the Old Lady there, watching TV in the living room. It was the first chance he had had to confront her.

"All these years you cursed the father who gave me life. You made me feel like a bastard, because I didn't know who my father was. And then when I get the chance to know him, just for a short time, the last few moments of his life, you take that chance away from me, without even telling me..."

The Old Lady nodded wearily. It was the first time Zukie had used such an angry tone to her and he had every right to. She had done him wrong.

"You used me to get back at him," Zukie continued. "You could have told me he was dying. You coulda told me he wanted to see me. I wanted to know him."

"Zukie, I'm sorry," the Old Lady said meekly. "But whatever I say can't give you what I've taken away from you. But you have to understand, Zukie, I was filled with so much hate for so many years..."

Zukie was raging inwardly, but now when he saw his mother's eyes, pleading to him for forgiveness, he realised that for the first time in his life, he had power over the Old Lady and it made him feel uncomfortable.

STORM SUDDENLY SNAPPED awake. He'd been dreaming. Again.

His hands searched for the 9mm Beretta under the cushion. He found it. He took the gun out and looked at it, turning it over and over in his hand. It was a powerful weapon, but he was not as comfortable with it as he was with his Browning 9mm Hi-Power. He decided he would swap them over later .

He'd fallen asleep watching the TV, which was now a fuzzy screen. He switched it off with the remote control.

Dressed only in a pair of white undershorts, he headed upstairs to check on Jazzy and Lee.

Lee was curled foetally in his bed, his duvet thrown off, toys scattered about on the floor. His favourite 'Gladiator', Shadow the invincible muscleman, smiled down at him from the poster on the wall. As Storm covered Lee with the duvet, he wondered what dreams haunted his little boy as his head tossed from side to side in his sleep. Did he see masked men with guns raging at him? He bent down and kissed his son tenderly on the forehead. Then he thought about his half-brother, Eugene. He had recognised him as a Piper man. The boy must have known who he was. He wondered if the realisation was as much a dilemma for Eugene as it was for him. What would Eugene do about his discovery.

Jasmine's breath rose steadily as he stood in the bedroom doorway and watched her. Even in her sleep, she maintained her elegance and beauty. Half of him wanted to climb into bed with her there and then, while the other half warned him to stay clear. As if sensing his presence, she stirred awake. He heard the fear in her voice.

"Cliff? Is that you? Is everything okay?"

"Yeah, everything's okay. Go back to sleep."

Downstairs in the kitchen, he paused to think. A strange feeling clung to him, like a shiver down his spine. He pulled a sweater over his naked chest, but he still felt it. He went across to the kitchen counter and made himself some strong black coffee, but didn't have a chance to drink it before he heard the sound of his mobile phone ringing. It was Lewty again, explaining what was going on out on the streets. He sounded impatient and weary. Storm explained that he needed to lie low for a while longer. It was too complicated to discuss over the phone.

"What the fuck do you think this is?" Lewty asked angrily. "Play school or something?"

Storm tried to calm him, assuring him that everything was planned. He was just giving Jigsy enough rope to hang himself.

"And time longer than rope," he added.

BLUEBWAI REPEATEDLY SWITCHED the TV channels over, not looking for any programme in particular.

He yawned, lying on his back, his bare feet on the comfortable sofa. Sleep pulled at his eyelids. He was just beginning to drift off when his mother stormed into the living room.

"Why haven't you done any of the cleaning?!" she shouted. "I'm sick of being treated like your personal housemaid. Since your father died, you haven't been

185

pulling your weight around here and I'm not having it. And take your feet of the sofa!"

Bluebwai raised himself slightly, reached for the superior remote control unit and proceeded to turn the volume up, drowning out his mother's voice.

She stood staring in total bewilderment. In a fury, she went to the back of the box and pulled out the plug. The television died. She glared at her son. The boy remained passive.

"How dare you?!" his mother shrieked, her face distorted with anger. "You didn't behave like this when Vermont was alive."

The look that her son threw her made her body grow cold. Bluebwai kissed his teeth with subdued aggression. His mother threw up her hands in frustration. How did her son become this way, her baby Eugene who used to be so quiet and timid had, little by little, become someone else. He always had to walk in a certain way or talk in a certain way, and he had a bad attitude. She hardly recognised the real Eugene in him anymore. He had become more secretive. He often stayed out all night long and the few times he was at home, he would keep to himself, locked inside his bedroom.

"Eugene, what's wrong with you?" she said, almost pleading.

"Nothing's wrong with me," Blue muttered. "Just get off my case." He got up to a sitting position.

"Don't I know my son?" his mother asked.

"Yeah, like you know your bottle of gin."

She chose to ignore the insulting remarks.

"Eugene, you've been behaving really odd since your

186

father's funeral. Now what is it? I've never seen you in such a dark mood before." She paused thoughtfully. "Is it me? Is it something I've said or done?"

"You shoulda told me about them before!" he suddenly yelled at her. "Why didn't you tell me before?"

His mother sat there blinking. The question threw her concentration off balance. She didn't know what to say. "Eugene, I, I..." She reached out towards him. Bluebwai dismissed her with a wave of his hand and went and stood over by the fireplace, as far from her as he could get in the same room.

"You knew. Why didn't you tell me?"

"It didn't seem important... I mean, you didn't know them and I had no reason to believe you'd ever meet them. Vermont wanted them at the funeral. Wanted you to get to know them. If it was up to me they wouldn't have been there."

Bluebwai swung around and glared at her.

"They're my flesh and blood too, Mum. My own flesh and blood."

"Eugene, I understand how you feel."

"What are you talking about?" Bluebwai sneered. "How could you?"

He jammed his hands in his jeans pockets, looking down at his feet. He let out a sigh. "I'm outta here. Gonna get a place of my own. I'm leaving in a couple of days."

His mother looked horrified, as if paralysed as a steam roller rumbled towards her.

"Eugene, you're all I have." He could see the tears threatening. "Eugene, why?"

"I don't belong here."

"Eugene, this is your home. It's always been your home. How can you say that to me? What's making you say these things?"

"Mum, I'm a big boy now. I can find my own way in the world."

"Where will you go?" she said, fighting back tears.

"Dunno," he said, with a shrug of his shoulders. "Don't worry, Mum, things will be easier for you when I leave."

She looked at him questioning.

"It's no big secret, is it?" he asked. "I know you tried hard for me, too hard. You say you want me to be a lawyer or a doctor. But I'll never be what you want me to be, because really you want me to be white. Since my dad died there's been no reason for me to stay here. Your family have never accepted me. Too dark for white, yeah? I may as well be going."

He said he had already packed his things.

"I don't understand. Why do have to go so soon?" his mother asked as she crossed shakily to the drink's cabinet to pour herself a gin.

Bluebwai looked across at his mother, a scowl on his face. Why? What is this? She had to be fucking crazy. He had just discovered that he had two brothers, who he definitely didn't want. He knew who Clifton was and he didn't want anything to do with him. 'Why fucking me?' he asked himself. 'This is crazy. No raas way!' Jigsy was more like his brother than Storm. Fuck! Jigsy...! Supposing he put two and two together and worked it out? He'd better pray that Jigsy didn't find out that Storm was his half-brother. It was a crisis situation and Bluebwai was feeling it.

THINGS DEFINITELY LOOKED different in daylight. Zukie was fooled into thinking that it was safer than night time. He needed to see Paradise by any means necessary. He made his way up the gravel path towards Pastor Browne's house, wearing a baggy, dark green denim outfit and ankle boots. The rottweillers barked at him ferociously, tugging at their leashes to get one, just one, bite of this intruder. Fortunately, they were well chained and Zukie was able to stay just clear of the length of leash. A sudden movement registered at the corner of his eye. Looking towards the house, he saw Mona Browne at the window, a look of pure horror manifested on her face. Then she disappeared. His heart leapt wildly with excitement.

The front door swung open quickly, and Mona Browne was staring aghast at the dreadlocked boy as he approached the step.

"You!" she cried angrily. "How dare you!" Mona Browne scowled. "You have the audacity to show your face at our door again. How dare you!"

Zukie studied the woman before him and wondered why she was giving him all this grief. Either way he wasn't going to leave without finding out where Paradise was.

"I don't come to check you, yuh know, Mrs Browne. Me come fe check yuh daughter!"

Mona couldn't believe his impudence.

"Look, you're trespassing. This is private property. If you don't leave immediately, I'll call the police."

"Call the blasted police!" Zukie yelled at her, tired of all the pussyfooting around. "Maybe they can shed some light on what unuh done with Paradise."

"They haven't done anything with me," came Paradise's voice from inside the house, behind her mother. She appeared on the doorstep and stood smiling at Zukie. For a moment, he didn't know what to say. He wanted to hold her, caress her, kiss her face all over, and whisper sweet nothings in her ear. He wanted her to hold him to her breast and lull him into a deep and dreamless sleep. But as he made a move towards her, her mother stepped in between and held her ground, arms folded, her eyes warning him that he would caress her daughter, 'over my dead body'.

"Mrs B.," Zukie said boldly, "yuh cyan stop me seeing Paradise. I need her right now."

Mona smiled a nervous smile. Paradise ignored her and sidestepped her mother to reach Zukie. She walked slowly towards him, swinging her arms slightly, her cherry-red lips parted slightly in a smile. Zukie thought she looked stunning in her simple, front-buttoned, full length, black denim skirt and cream-coloured knitted top. She looked into his eyes lovingly and held his face in her hands, then gently kissed him on the lips.

For an instant Mona stood there, her mouth agape, her eyes wide. Realising there was nothing she could do, she stepped back inside her house, kicking the door shut behind her.

Now that they were alone, the words didn't come together. They looked playfully in each other's eyes. Paradise took him by the hand and they walked around to the large, landscaped garden at the back of the house. Her eyes seemed joyful, but still she said nothing. He wondered whether those eyes were laughing at him, whether this was some kind of game. Maybe Paradise was leading him to another beating. Maybe Pastor Browne would be lying in wait for him amongst the bushes.

"Oh Zukie," Paradise sighed, "what are we going to do with each other?"

"What do you mean?"

"Well, you've been thrown out of your house and my dad will kill you if he catches you in our house again."

"What's his problem anyway?" Zukie asked.

"That's a good question," Paradise laughed. She was wondering the very same thing herself. No boy who took an interest in her was ever good enough in his eyes. He always found something to dislike about them. He was now saying he didn't want any dreadlocks man seeing his daughter. That's why he had sent her away to a strict aunt in Leeds, after he stumbled on Zukie and Paradise in their moment of passion. He wanted to keep her as far away from Zukie as possible. And he believed that only this fundamentalist aunt could put the fear of God back into his daughter.

"It's none of his business," said Zukie.

"It is if I live in his house," Paradise replied. "We've got nowhere where we can be... you know... together."

"You can stay over by Chico's mum one night if you want to. He's hardly ever there and his mum goes to bed early."

"Are you sure?" Paradise asked seriously. "You sure she won't mind?"

" 'Course I'm sure. And if you don't want to stay here at your dad's that's alright as well. We could get a place together. I've got to get a more permanent place and I don't mind sharing with you."

A glint lit up in Paradise's eyes. Whether Zukie was aware of it or not, she was reading behind the lines and interpreted Zukie's offer as a declaration of intent.

If truth be told, Zukie was boldly making promises he could not guarantee to honour. Yeah, Chico was hardly ever in, but knowing him, he would show up on the very night she was there. And sure, Chico's mother went to bed early, but he didn't know how Sister Anthony would take it if she discovered that the pastor's daughter was cavorting with her lodger under her roof. As for being able to share a flat with Paradise, where was he going to get the money for the deposit or the month's rent in advance? He would consider all these things later, but right now he was floating on love's light wings and believed there was nothing he couldn't do.

"Look Zuchael Michaels, I don't know if you're serious. I hope you are. Because I am. I've always had a crush on you. Even when we were kids. But don't feel you have to say those things to make me happy. Don't say anything to me unless you mean it."

Paradise's mother called from behind the back door, her voice anxious.

"Please ask your companion to leave. Your father will be home soon and I don't think he would be too pleased to..."

Zukie had run out of time. He told Paradise where to meet him and when.

"I think I love you," he whispered before parting. "I think I know I love you. You already know that, don't you?"

Paradise said she hoped he did and begged him to hurry.

Before departing, Zukie added: "We'll get a cheap flat, slightly run down and we'll do it up ourselves. We'll paint the whole flat white. What do you think?"

THE OFFICERS DIDN'T bother to knock. They had staked the place all night and moved in as soon as Bow-Bow and Pee-Wee left the house. They had to move fast so, they kicked the back door in with their guns at the ready. The bolt on the inside easily came away from the rotten wood which framed the door.

Since Bow-Bow had embarrassed the department in court, the order had gone out to bring Bow-Bow in on a long-stretch offence. That way he would be forced to make a deal from which he would find it more difficult to renege. All they wanted him to do was testify against Jigsy. The Manchester police knew that Marvin Ellis was a key member of the Piper Mill gang and linked him with a lot of the gang violence in Moss Side. But they couldn't pin anything on him because everybody was too afraid to testify. After Bow-Bow was bludgeoned almost to death, it was easy to convince him that he would be doing society and himself a favour if Ellis was put away for a very long time. Somehow Ellis got to him before the trial and convinced him otherwise, despite the police protection they offered Bow-Bow. This time they were going to get him, no mistake and this time Bow-Bow would co-operate in nailing Ellis. This time they were going to turn him informer. They knew that he was feeding a habit, and like every coke head, always had a little bit stashed away for an emergency.

Detective Constables Colin Edwards and Barry Hodge spent hours examining every room in the house, every potential hiding place, every crack in the wall. The more they snooped around, the more their frustration intensified. It wouldn't go down too well down at the nick if the house was clean, yet every corner they looked in came up dry. They whispered their suspicions to each other. "Maybe Bow-Bow got wind of us and got rid of any evidence."

As the detectives were about to give up the search on Bow-Bow's home, the phone rang. They looked at each other nervously. Edwards made the decision quick. He picked up the phone and answered in his best muffled imitation of Bow-Bow's voice.

"Hello, is that you, Delroy?" Edwards recognised the voice.

"Yeah. Pee-Wee?"

"Do you want me to bring the stuff over?"

"Yeah. Yeah bring it."

"Alright then," the woman concluded. "I'm coming over."

STORM RECEIVED A call on his mobile. It was Lalah. "Please get over here right away," she said to him. "It's an emergency."

Storm sped over to the hospital in his car, worried that something had happened to Tia. When he raced into the ward he got the shock of his life — both Jazzy and Lalah were waiting for him.

"Oh shit!" he cried out loud. For a moment he debated what to do: head for cover or face the music. He turned to Jazzy who was boiling with anger. He saw the rage in her eyes. Why hadn't he told her about Lalah and the baby? It was her friend, a nurse at the hospital who, to her surprise, spotted him when he came at visiting times. She mentioned it to Jazzy thinking it was probably something she already knew about. All this time he was coming to her house for comfort because his other woman was in hospital. Storm looked away. It wasn't the first time he'd been confronted by a furious girlfriend, but then he turned to Lalah who looked at him just as angrily. She had suspected something. He had been coming to visit at the hospital smelling of all kinds of perfume, and too tired to not have been up to anything.

"Make a choice right now," Lalah demanded. He turned to Jazzy, then back to Lalah

"Now," Lalah insisted, "you heartless bastard!"

He looked at Jazzy, shrugging his shoulders. "I want Lalah," he said quietly.

Jazzy turned and walked out. Lalah looked away. The question in her heart was did she want him?

LIKE MOST OF the Grange people, Colours was incensed at the liberties Storm was allowing the Pipers to get away with. He hadn't spent six months down at D.C. only to let some pussyhole from Piper Mill run things. What the fuck was Storm playing at with his disappearing act? In the middle of a crisis and all. Nobody had seen him for more than two weeks. He could only be contacted on his mobile phone, and even then he was unable to make any concrete decision about how they would deal with the Pipers. His attitude was, "let's just wait and see", even when the Pipers had brazenly shot-up their Shabba dance and robbed them. Colours took that one as a personal insult. His baby mother was one of the ravers in the venue and she could have easily been caught in the crossfire. What then? No, the Pipers were going to pay for all their slackness. Even if it meant taking the matter in his own hands. And to make matters worse, their second-in-command, Lewty, seemed to have slacked too. No one had seen him. Meanwhile Rough was lying in a critical condition in hospital and the crew were standing around looking like shit.

Colours parked up around the corner from the

nearest hamburger restaurant. He was hungry. Frenchie, in the passenger seat, agreed that food was a good idea. Lick-Shot, in the back seat, said, "That makes three of us." They climbed out of the car and disappeared around the corner, discussing whether it was better to get a Quarter Pounder with cheese or a fillet of fish, fries, with a Coke and a piece of apple pie.

Like Teeko, Colours was a martial arts freak from a young age, and though he no longer competed, he made sure that he kept his fitness up. Colours met Teeko years ago when they faced each other at a karate tournament. They couldn't have been more than fourteen, but Colours had never forgotten Teeko's gold ring with his initials T.K., Terry Kelly. The youth had run up his mouth so much when the tournament judges insisted that he remove the ring before he fought. Teeko had insisted that it couldn't come off, but it finally did when the judges threatened a disqualification.

Standing at the counter to place their orders, Colours eyed a burly guy whose face looked remarkably like the young Teeko he once knew. Colours focused his eyes intently. Back then, Teeko used to have an afro. Despite the shaven head and the extra weight, he reminded Colours too much of Teeko for his liking. He looked at the youth's hand. The ring was there.

"Hey, Teeko!" Colours called nonchalantly.

The baldheaded youth turned quickly and looked at him, a vague look of recognition on his face, but clearly he couldn't work out where from.

"No, I ain't Teeko," he said eventually. "I'm his brother."

Colours wouldn't take his eyes off the larger man.

"No... bullshit Mister Handman. I know you, you're fucking Teeko," Colours insisted, pointing his finger at the ring. "You're definitely Teeko, man."

A trickle of sweat appeared on Teeko's forehead as he saw the three youths in front of him, all feeling for their guns. He picked up his order and slowly edged his way towards the exit.

"No, you've got the wrong bloke. Believe me, you've got the wrong bloke."

The three Grange youths followed him slowly as he backed out.

"Hey, Teeko, you've put on weight, man. What's the matter, don't you go training no more?" Colours smiled, a cruel smile. "Yuh is big belly man, now."

"I told you, I'm not Teeko!" the youth insisted, his voice hoarse.

The youth edged closer and closer to the door until he was close enough to make his getaway. Without warning, he threw his entire order of fries, hamburger and milkshake into the path of the approaching Grange boys and made a rush for the door.

Colours was after him like a bullet, while Lick-Shot and Frenchie brought up the rear, keeping their weapons concealed. They ran through the city centre, knocking pedestrians over and narrowly avoiding cars and trams as they chased after Teeko. The Piper youth kept running and running as if his life depended on it. His life *did* depend on it. The Grange had more than one reason to seek revenge on him. He ran and ran, out of the city centre and up a busy road in the direction of Cheetham Hill. Colours was wrong about his training. Teeko still trained regularly and was a good runner

198

despite his heavy frame. He was far from his neighbourhood, but right now he didn't care. He just wanted to get clear. He turned around. They were still behind him. He decided to lose them by going off the road. His chance came up when he saw the gates of a deserted factory, set back from the road a bit. He scaled the fence on his first attempt, and was about to jump over on the other side and lose himself in the factory's maze of rooms, when he heard Colours' voice say menacingly:

"Teeko, don't even think of moving or I'll blow your fuckin' head off!"

Sitting on top of the fence with ripples of sweat forming on the top of his shaven head, Teeko looked down at the gun pointed at him. He twitched slightly as if still undecided whether he should make a run for it anyway.

"Stay where the fuck you are!" Frenchie shouted, his gun also drawn and pointing up at Teeko.

"Him haffe hol' one corn!" Lick-Shot insisted as he finally arrived, out of breath and with his gun drawn. "Him mus' tek at least one corn for all the running."

Without warning, Teeko, the dedicated karate student who loved testing what he learned at school in the field, pounced down on Colours from the top of the fence, with his arms swinging wildly, and directed a well-aimed kick at Colours' head. Colours wasn't expecting it and it happened too quickly for him to do anything about it. He let out a cry of pain as Teeko landed directly on top of him, throwing him to the ground.

The two youths wrestled on the ground furiously,

neither wanting to give way, rolling over and over again. Frenchie and Lick-Shot looked at each other, undecided about what to do. They knew Colours could handle himself on a one to one situation and anyway, with both of them rolling around on the ground so fast, they couldn't be sure of getting a clear hit at Teeko without hitting Colours.

Somehow, Colours managed to struggle up to his feet and proceeded to blast his opponent with a series of right hooks. Teeko fought back, trading punch for punch. Then they gripped each other by the necks, each one trying to get an advantage over the other. Suddenly, Teeko opened his mouth and sunk his teeth deep into Colours' arm and ripped away at Colours' flesh. Colours screamed in agony, "You motherfucker!" While his opponent howled in pain, Teeko took the opportunity to make a run for it, back to the roadside, as fast as he could, in a zig-zagging motion. Lick-Shot fired a couple of shots in his direction, just over his head, but Teeko ignored them completely and just kept running. Praying none of the bullets hit home.

THE FRONT DOOR was wide open, swinging in the wind. The floor in the hallway was carpetless.

"Jasmine? Jazzy?" Storm knew she had gone. He'd only said what he did at the hospital to save face. The truth was he loved and respected Jasmine. He didn't mean to use or humiliate her. He was coming back to explain. But it was too late, Jazzy had gone. He stepped into the house. There was no furniture. A note was pinned to the kitchen door. Jasmine's neat handwriting flowed off the page.

Dear Clifton,

I've lost the Cliff that I once loved. But that is only one of the reasons why I have taken Lee. Please don't try to find us. Lee will miss you, but it's better this way. I always hoped that one day we would be like a real family. But those things were never going to happen.

Lee and I are the disappointed ones. We didn't feature in your life as we should have. Still, there's nothing we can do about all that now. Goodbye. Jazzy.

Storm re-read the note frantically unable to believe that she had stolen Lee from him, like a thief in the night. They were gone. He screwed the letter up, throwing it aside and sank slowly to the floor, his head in his hands. A solitary tear rolled down his cheek out of sadness and despair.

His mobile phone began to ring. He allowed it to carry on ringing. A strange feeling crept over him. The phone stopped. Clifton looked at it solemnly, surprised at how calm he felt. In a way it was a relief that she was gone. Now he would have more time to concentrate on Jigsy.

PEE-WEE SAT down on the settee, aware that she had

fucked up. She had fucked up big time. After calling Bow-Bow in the house, she had reached back to find the two detectives waiting for her with big smiles on their faces. Worst of all she was carrying a quantity of pure coke on her. A quantity even she knew was large enough to guarantee a long, custodial sentence.

As soon as she realised her mistake, she quickly turned and made a run for it, her instinct for survival sharpened. But he was faster and fitter. The black cop chased after her and rugby-tackled her down to the ground. Even then, she didn't give up. Edwards found himself fighting with her. She bit him hard on the hand as he tried to restrain her. He howled with pain. She bit so hard, her teeth penetrated flesh. He had underestimated her, but nevertheless his power was far superior to hers and it didn't take him long to restrain her. He decided not to take any more chances and dragged her viciously, hauling her back into Bow-Bow's house, screaming and spitting, taking care that no part of him was anywhere near her snarling mouth.

Later, when they had her under manners, and after he had bandaged his injured hand, Edwards teased her saying, "Bow-Bow sends his apology for not being here to personally share this moment with you."

"What frigging moment?" she hissed.

"Okay, enough of the slackness," Edwards said, caressing his injured hand. "Is there anything you want to tell us?"

"Yeah, right," she said scowling. "I don't know nothing, right."

Edwards turned to his partner smiling. They knew they had hit the jackpot. They could see the fear in Pee-

Wee's eyes. She was probably as worried about the reaction from Bow-Bow when he discovered that they had lost this amount of merchandise. There must have been nearly half a kilo of coke there. They must have been planning something big. Yeah, Edwards thought to himself, this time Bow-Bow's gonna sing like a bird.

A WHITE DOVE. Beautiful, pure, innocent. Flying frantically around in The Old Lady's living room. Trapped. A symbol of peace. But how did it get in? Storm looked around, but all the windows were closed. How did it get in?

Storm watched fascinated, as the bird swooped and dived, panicking, circling, trying to find a way out.

Outside, a green-turbaned Jigsy was peering in through the window, laughing. In his hand he held a small handgun. He took aim, firing with precision. The bird dropped like a stone. Scattering feathers everywhere, blood splashing the walls

Storm woke up panting heavily, sweating, clutching his hair. A dream. Only a dream. Leaping from the bed, he snatched his watch off the bedside table.

He had slept for two hours. Longer than he intended. Outside it was still dark. Storm's heart hammered in his chest.

IT WAS ANOTHER hour before Bow-Bow arrived home. They were sitting in the rear living room, waiting for him, the two detectives with their guns drawn and tense from all the suspense, and Pee-Wee, handcuffed on the settee on which, the previous evening, she had enjoyed a pleasurable, if brief, romp with Bow-Bow. They heard the key turn in the lock, heard the door close. They heard Bow check another room and call out for Pee-Wee. And they heard him approaching the closed door of the room they were in.

"Surprise!" Edwards shouted as the door opened and Bow-Bow's diminutive figure stepped in the living room.

Bow-Bow froze on the spot, threw his hands up high and looked across at his girlfriend, lying trussed up on the settee. At first he thought it was a gang raid, but the combination of one white man and one black man, both waving guns in his face and assuming the same stance, confused him. He thought he recognised the black man. But he had never seen the white man before in his life. He was sure of that.

"Police!" Edwards announced, waving his warrant card in his bandaged hand.

"Aaah fuck it!" Bow-Bow cursed. "What do you fuckers want this time?"

"We want you, Bow-Bow."

"What the fuck am I s'posed to have done this time?"

Edwards produced the parcel of coke. "You should take better care of your merchandise, Bow," Edwards said, an ironic smile on his face.

Bow-Bow swallowed hard. He guessed what was in the parcel. It was worth a lot of money to him, but he

204

didn't think about the money he had just lost. All he could think of was that he was looking at a fucking long stretch if he went down for this. He would be a fucking old man before he came out.

"Yeah, right," he said, nervously, "you're trying to frame me, you're always trying to frame me. I'm innocent!"

BLUEBWAI STEPPED OUT of his mother's house dressed in a hooded, khaki parka, woolly hat and baggy denim jeans. His mind was swirling with thoughts. He was so lost in his thinking he didn't hear the soft purr of a car engine coming down the street behind him. As it neared, the car horn sounded. Bluebwai turned around quickly, still a bit jumpy. The Jag pulled up beside him.

Jigsy was grinning impetuously behind the wheel. Easy-Love sat in the passenger seat, looking up and down the road cautiously. The window at the passenger's side wound down and Easy stuck his head out.

"What's happening, rudebwai? How you so jumpy? Settle nuh, you look like a duppy fe real."

Beside him, Jigsy threw back his green-turbaned head and laughed, savouring the joke.

"I didn't know it was you," Bluebwai muttered, walking over, his heart pumping so fast, he could almost feel the blood racing around his body.

"Come soon, come soon, starbwai," Jigsy said. "Just cool."

Jigsy kept the engine running and told Blue to step in the car. The boy obeyed, opened the rear door and climbed in. Jigsy looked around at the houses on the street.

"Yeah, nice street you got here, Blue. Quiet neighbourhood, the way I like it," said Easy.

"So what's happening, yout'?" Jigsy asked, glancing back at Blue in the rearview mirror. "Easy was worried about you. Been trying to call you on your mobile. Mek sure everything was alright."

"Yeah, everything's alright," Bluebwai declared quietly. "My pops died. Just got a lot of things on my mind, yuh know."

Jigsy nodded. "Yeah, it's rough when your people die. I know how you're feeling, homes. Where you off to now?"

"Going?" Bluebwai feigned ignorance. "I was just strolling, nowhere special... Just needed to get out of the house. Mum driving me up the wall. Well, you know how mothers stay, innit?"

"So tell me somet'ing," Easy asked, "yuh 'ave a sister? Yuh know how me love dem redskin gyal!"

Blue frowned. He shook his head.

"Cousin?" Easy asked hopefully.

Blue shook his head again. "In't got nobody now my pops is gone. Just me and my mum."

"Pity," Easy said, regretfully.

"Don't mind him," Jigsy said to Blue." Stop your jesting, Easy man. You can see the bwai don't like it. Come Bluebwai, we waste 'nuff time a'ready. I've got an important job to do for real and I want you in on it."

Jigsy shifted the gear into drive and the Jag pulled away with a roar.

"What is it?" Blue asked anxiously, as they drove on. "What's the job? Where is it?"

"Don't worry," Easy replied, pulling out a compact Uzi from the canvas sports holdall in front of him. "We'll show you." He handed Blue the Uzi. "All you got to do is ride shotgun."

LEWTY PROUDLY ADMIRED his new, high performance BMW convertible parked outside the youth centre on the estate. This was what he had always wanted. A car to pose in and a car that enabled him to take off whenever he needed to get far, far away from the life he was living.

The warm, soapy water bubbled over the deep blue paintwork. The two kids washed the car lovingly, their mountain bikes lying on the pavement beside it. Lewty was paying them to give his car a wash and wax and they were only too happy to oblige. It was only late afternoon, but it was already getting dark. Lewty glanced at his Raymond Weil watch. It was only five. He couldn't wait until the summer came around when he would really be able to drive with the top down.

Jigsy drove around the park a couple of times, then turned down a side street. Finally, he decided to go up by the youth centre. As they pulled into the estate, Easy-

Love spotted Lewty from behind, admiring his car. He prodded Jigsy.

"There's the G boy. Lewty the tooty. See him deh."

Jigsy bolted upright. A cold look on his face, he eased the Jaguar forward at a slow crawl, heading straight for Lewty up ahead.

Lewty had finally arranged to meet Colours, Lick-Shot and Frenchie outside the Cowesby Street blues. They knew that Jigsy usually frequented the place. Colours had a plan. With Storm having gone A.W.O.L., Lewty was interested to hear Colours' suggestions.

At seventeen, Lewty was already 'second-in-command' of the Grange crew, had more money than he knew what to do with, and earned respect in most places. Storm trusted him completely. Lewty always attended to his duties diligently and Storm knew him as an intelligent and fearless youth, totally loyal to the Grange. He was young, but experienced in street runnings. A smooth operator.

Lewty zipped up his suede parka. A car alarm was blaring somewhere on the estate. He told the kids washing his car to speed it up. He had to go soon.

The car was almost behind him when the horn sounded. Lewty turned his head casually and faced a trio of Pipers, one of them with a green bandanna wrapped around his head, all brandishing weapons out of the Jag window.

"Shit!" he exclaimed. "I don't believe it."

"Neither do we," Easy-Love laughed, waving a pump-action shotgun at Lewty. "Neither do we... Lewty, how ya doing?"

209

Lewty looked at Easy-Love and smiled uneasily. His eyes were fixed on the nervous-looking kid hanging out of the rear window waving an Uzi.

"Lewty," Jigsy said wryly, fixing the Grange man with a bloodshot stare, "I have good news and bad news. The good news is, I'm gonna let the kids go. The bad news is you're coming with us."

The two youths who had been washing Lewty's car began fidgeting, both reluctant to abandon their friend like this, but aware that they were no match for guns. Lewty told them to go. Still unsure, they backed off and climbed on their bikes.

"You gotta come with us," Easy repeated, enjoying it all.

The Pipers stepped out of the car, cautiously. Lewty tightened his grip, clenching his teeth.

Face to face, and with his gun pointed at the Grange youth, Jigsy headbutted him squarely on the bridge of his nose. "You're invited to dinner," he snarled. "Never turn down a Piper invitation. Especially when *you're* on the fucking menu!"

Lewty went down but struggled back to his feet, blood streaming out of both nostrils. He grabbed onto his assailants green turban out of desperation, pulling it off his head. Jigsy headbutted him a second time, then a third time. Lewty crashed to the ground, but again struggled to get up, but his legs were weak and his head too groggy to co-ordinate them. He was hurting badly, but summoned all his strength to make it look like nothing. Then Jigsy's boot smashed into his face and, this time, Lewty stayed down, groaning in pain. For the first time in his life, Lewty had lost a fight.

IN THE INTERVIEW room, the cassette recorder was rolling. Bow-Bow looked pissed off and tired. He wasn't in the mood. He had been through police interviews so many times before and they still pissed him off. The cops took liberties and kept asking questions until you were so tired you were prepared to say anything, just as long as they let you sleep a while.

Bow-Bow had already been charged with possession and conspiracy. Pee-Wee willingly signed a statement implicating her boyfriend. His solicitor advised that it looked bad. When the offer of the deal came through, Bow-Bow had no choice but to take it. Now they were asking him everything about all the recent gang-banging going down. They asked about the shootings and who was controlling which turf. For the second time in his short life, Delroy 'Bow-Bow' Watkins became a reluctant police informer and he knew what the consequences would be for him out on the streets. But he was looking at ten or twelve years or maybe more. That was a prospect more frightening than all the 'Jigsy's' in the world.

"I don't know who's doing all the shooting," Bow-Bow said defensively. "All I know is that the Grange and the Pipers are fighting for turf. That's all I know, man. I don't get involved with gangs, man."

Detective Hodge didn't believe him, but gave him enough rope.

"Are you saying that you are totally innocent?" he

asked taking off his green bomber jacket and hanging it on the back of his chair.

Bow-Bow looked at the officer. Could he really be so stupid, he wondered.

"Yeah, that's right!" Bow-Bow said, smiling. "Totally innocent."

"Then how comes there was an attempt on your life earlier this year? Why would anybody want to kill an innocent man?"

Bow-Bow looked mystified. Why was this bloke going over old ground? "Like I said in court, I don't know why. It was a case of mistaken identity... Look, I was bad when I was younger, I in't scared to admit it. I used to get into a lot of fights and things like that. But I'm not with that stuff no more, man. I'm trying to better myself now."

"Come on, Delroy, are you or are you not a member of the Cheetham Hill Panthers gang?"

Bow-Bow simply kissed his teeth and said "Cho'!"

WHILE HIS PARTNER was questioning Watkins down at the station, Detective Constable Colin Edwards remained in Bow-Bow's house in the hope that the youth was working with others and he would be able to trap them all in his net. Bow-Bow had to be working with someone. He knew most of the players on the scene and how they operated. He knew that Bow-Bow had gone underground after changing his court testimony against Jigsy. As far as Edwards could make out, Bow-Bow wasn't even getting help from his Cheetham Hill Panthers. Half a ki of pure grade cocaine was too much to shift for someone operating on his own.

It had been three long days now, but Edwards reminded himself that all he had to do was be patient and he would get results.

He had a lot of time on his hands. Fortunately, Pee-Wee had a number of women's magazines in the bathroom. Edwards read them voraciously as there was nothing else to read in the entire house, not a single book or newspaper or any other magazine. All the time he had his handgun beside him.

Guns were fairly routine in drug busts, because so many of the dealers out there were just crazy. Since crack emerged as the number one drug, the stakes were high. In certain areas, it was difficult to find anybody who was just quietly selling their sticks of weed. With the stakes so high, the risks got higher and, because the risks got higher, the protection got heavier, and both the guilty and the innocent were getting caught in the crossfire. He had seen so many youths killed before their time. He was even at the scene of Fluxy's murder. A pool of dried, clotted blood on the pavement was all that marked the spot where he was slain. A double shotgun blast to the chest had ended his young life. Death in the afternoon.

And being black, Edwards' superiors always threw him in the thick of things, as if the gang violence in Manchester was his personal problem. A couple of serious attempts had already been made on his life and he feared there would be more. He was a hero nobody knew about.

Edwards sighed as he reflected. Sometimes he didn't know how he was supposed to do his job as a law enforcement officer with all the madness on the streets, or how he was expected to protect the community, or even if his small role in the big picture was doing any good.

He went through the same routine each of the three days he was in Bow-Bow's house. In the mornings he would read the magazines, in the afternoon he would check in with his partner to see how Bow-Bow's questioning was going down. And in the evening he chilled. Unable to sleep, his gun at his side, he would stare at the television all night and into the morning, listening for passing cars or unannounced guests. Edwards felt empty, tired, drained. Why the fuck were black youths always blasting each other? Things weren't supposed to go down like this. Okay, if you're a villain, fine. Or if you want to make a show of strength or carry out a straightforward robbery. But why did the Moss Side crews always have to come out with their fingers on the trigger, blasting. Everywhere you looked kids, no more than fourteen or fifteen, were pulling out guns in wild shootouts in crowded areas, turning the neighbourhood into a war zone and leaving behind them a trail of grieving mothers, brothers, fathers, sisters, girlfriends and orphans. He had watched helplessly, as the neighbourhood of his childhood degenerated. He wanted to do something about it, but it felt like all he got from the community, his community, was a wall of silence, or a lot of abuse about being an 'Uncle Tom', a 'house nigga', a 'coconut'. He had heard it all. While he was on the frontline, risking his life trying to make the streets safe, trying to protect people's property, and putting dealers in jail, he was regarded as some kind of traitor to the cause.

He had made a thorough search of Bow-Bow's flat and hadn't come up with anything. And it was down to luck that he found the shotgun cartridge down the side of the sofa under the seat cushions. He picked it up carefully with his handkerchief and casually tucked it into his shirt pocket. He would have it analysed back at the station.

Edwards thought about his years on the Force, the years that had passed, the things he had achieved and what he hadn't achieved. He thought also about his two sons, who were still very young and the kind of world he wanted them to live in. What kind of Manchester would they inherit after him? Would they succeed or become bad bwais? Some day soon, they would have to walk the very same bullet-ridden streets. He had promised himself that he would do his best to make their lives as whole as he could, and he grimaced at the thought that he was losing the battle.

Suddenly, the phone rang. He jumped up. He let it ring a couple more times, then picked it up and tried to sound like he imagined Bow-Bow would sound.

"Yaow!"

"Bow-Bow? Easy. Yuh 'ave it?"

"Yeah man," Edwards answered. "Everyt'ing ready. Yuh waan pass by?"

"Nah man. No time. You jus' tek care ah de merchandise an' me will check you more time, seen?"

The line went dead.

215

LYING ON THE bed in his attic room at the Old Lady's house, Clifton wished he could wind back the clock to his school days, his junior school days when he was so happy. He remembered those days, long before they moved to the present house in Hulme, when he didn't seem to have a care in the world. From their tiny council flat on one of the sprawling estates flanking Moss Side, he journeyed to school every morning, joined by some classmates en route. At school he developed his keen interest in sports and spent a lot of time playing football, cricket and doing athletics. Perhaps he could have won a scholarship to an American college, if he hadn't spent so much time learning to survive in his neighbourhood. He even knew someone who had done that. He and Gary had been best friends at one point. They used to play football and cricket together. When he came to think of it, Storm couldn't remember what happened, why they stopped hanging around together.

With the Old Lady at work all day, the streets outside beckoned. Especially in the summer holidays, when he and a friend would go on adventures together, exploring the neighbourhood, seeing what the streets were all about. Pretty soon, he hooked up with some fellas who could tell him the right from the wrong things about the streets, or about life itself. They taught him that he had one thing against him in life and that was the colour of his skin. That was how society was set up, and that unless he set up something for himself as an independent, all he could look forward to were minimum wage jobs. And Clifton remembered that he started hanging out more with other kids with whom he would run around with after school, looking for rival gangs to compete with, in anything, whether in sport or fighting, or even shoplifting. He would spend as much time as he could, chilling with his new friends, even though he knew that the Old Lady would be there when he got home, waiting to give him a good hiding. Sometimes they would just hang around in the cafes, being taught how to take care of themselves by the older guys with more experience. Learning how to survive on the streets. Even before going to secondary school, little Clifton hung out with men who had been in jail and rapped with guys who had boxed for a world title. The young boy was a keen listener and always took their advice. "To survive you've got to know what to do and know what not to do," the older guys on the frontline were always saying. That was the best advice he had ever learned.

Meanwhile, things were always tight at home. Struggling to bring two boys up on her own, the Old Lady rarely had more than the bare minimum at home. The only exception being when it came to food which they always had an abundance of. Neither of the Michael's boys ever went hungry. However, the Old Lady always seemed to be paying bills. If it wasn't the rent, it was the gas, and if it wasn't the gas, it was the electricity. They didn't even have a phone at the time. And there was no money to fix a broken window either. So if Clifton and Zukie broke the window in their room while playing football, they would have to make do with a bit of cardboard over the window all winter. And if they broke the window in her room, they better not let her catch them!

Being poor didn't bother the young Clifton unduly. Not until he was thirteen or fourteen when all the other kids used to come to school dressed in the latest gear from the most expensive shops, while his regulation grey trousers were patched in several places. Even that he could have lived with. But he was dating by the time he was fourteen, checking girls. He sometimes needed a little money in his pocket, just so as he could treat his girl to the movies or something. Being broke was getting embarrassing. Hanging at all the right places, it wasn't long before Clifton got involved in a little hustling, then a little dealing then, 'boom', he was high rollin'. The money was definitely one of the reasons he got involved.

ONLY JIGSY, EASY and Bluebwai heard Lewty screaming in the cellar where they had locked him in with Easy-Love's pet pit bull terrier. The screams from within were the most chilling Blue had ever heard. He felt physically sick. He was unable to speak or move. His throat was dry, his head beating like a drum, his body tingling, yet he kept his composure. Jigsy and Easy joked together singing, *"guess who's coming to dinner, another Grangebwai!"*

When Jigsy concluded from Lewty's screams that the boy was ready to talk, he opened the cellar hatch and called the animal to him. The dog, dripping with blood from its jaws and clutching a piece of flesh with its fangs, withdrew almost sorrowfully. Jigsy was feeling generous. He would give Lewty another chance to tell him the information he needed.

BLOOD, EVERYWHERE BLOOD. Blood on his hands, on his feet, all over. Wet, cold, running scared. Bare feet running on cold wet concrete. Pounding feet in his ears. Tired. Darkness surrounding, laughter behind him. Jeers and taunts.

"Where you going, pretty bwai? Don't you want to save your friends? With a friend like you, they might as well die."

Crying, sobbing, his breath coming in deep heaves, he heard someone shout from behind him: "Come on, no loose ends, let's wrap it up." He heard the sound of a pump-action mechanism snapping. They were coming after him. He turned and saw them. Three of them, heavily armed, aiming their guns at him. "Count...backwards...slowly!" one of them hissed.

"No," he screamed, "please, don't shoot me."

"Die, die you raas claat."

"No! No! Naaaaawww!!!!"

The bullets penetrated his chest and his whole body felt like it was on fire. He found himself falling, gasping for air, desperately grasping.

There was no pain. Only a gentle throbbing in his head. Zukie lifted himself off the mattress in Chico's room. His stomach was crying out for food and he needed a cigarette.

SOMETIMES YOU WAKE up and just feel good about yourself. You look out the window and see the sun shining bright and you feel even better. Everything seems to be falling in place. You turn on the portable radio in the shower and the first tune that comes on is your favourite Bob Marley, followed by version after version of oldies, but goodies. And even though you know you can't hold a tune, you can't resist humming loudly to yourself as you spray yourself with your favourite perfumed deodorant.

Frontline Radio were playing old tunes. An old revival was playing. Storm listened to the words. They matched his mood:

It's best to rise with a smile on your face
Just like the sun all over the place.

It really was a beautiful morning, one of those days when nothing could go wrong. You felt like you could make a bet on an outsider and the horse would romp home in first place. One of those days when you definitely had to buy a lottery ticket, because any numbers you selected would win the jackpot. Storm felt

221

so good that the first thing he did, when he came downstairs for his breakfast, was to grab his mother by the waist and hug her tightly.

"Stop, Clifton," she slapped her son's hand playfully. "Yuh waan kill me?"

"I know you in't had no good hugging recently, Mum," Clifton teased. "It's just to show you how much I appreciate you."

That was how it had been when he was younger. He was always hugging the Old Lady. When did he stop doing that regularly? He couldn't remember. He had also forgotten why the hugs had stopped.

At least he felt good today. And he would feel this good every day from now on. Because he was no longer a bad bwai. He didn't want to lose Lalah and the baby the way he had lost Jazzy. It wasn't going to be easy, but he would resign his leadership of the Grange. Since making his decision, he had become a new man. It was like a great load had been lifted off his shoulders. He selected something casual, but expensive, to wear.

"You still takin' me shopping?" the Old Lady asked.

"Of course I am, Mum. Just let me know when you're ready."

Yes, Clifton was feeling 'on top of the world', he was 'maxin' and relaxin' ', everything felt 'copasetic'.

JIGSY FELT ANXIOUS and hot. His armpits were wet and he was aware of sweat trickling down from under his white, polka dot turban, onto his forehead. He felt agitated and his body was beginning to tremble. He hadn't slept in two days but his wild eyes suggested that it had been weeks. Jigsy needed some powder. "Let's have a smoke," he mumbled. "I need one."

"We've wasted enough time already." Easy-Love's voice was full of strained impatience. "I think we should start."

The uneasy feeling clung close to Jigsy. He knew it was going to be the end of the road for someone. A sigh formed in his chest and stayed there. He gazed emptily out of the car window, casually taking in the scenery, the rows and rows of terraced housing, a far cry from his luxurious apartment in the Salford Quays Complex. Jigsy thought of Fluxy, and how much he missed his brother's company.

The atmosphere in the Jag was tense. Jigsy lit a cigarette quickly, turning slightly to look at Bluebwai in the back seat. The young boy turned his head and looked out of his window, an Uzi resting carelessly on his lap.

Bluebwai could feel Jigsy's probing eyes on him, but he continued gazing out the window, his mind lost in a thousand other thoughts. They had been up all night and he was exhausted. Right now, he could think of nowhere he'd rather be than in his bed at home, dozing off.

Yeah, the kid's safe, Jigsy thought. He had respect for Bluebwai and felt the boy possessed leadership qualities. Fluxy had felt the same way. He had trusted Bluebwai completely. In this thing, you develop a sense of who to trust. Call it instinct, but Jigsy was sure that the boy was going to achieve great things one day.

"Man alright," Jigsy said to Easy beside him, jerking his head back in Blue's direction.

"Yeah man," Easy agreed, "dat yout' cool an' deadly." He turned and smiled back at Blue reassuringly.

Jigsy turned up the music. Bad Bwai Buju Banton was on the wire bawling, in his rusty, raw voice:

Murderer, blood is on your shoulder
Kill I today, you cannot kill I tomorrow
Murderer, your insides must be hollow
How does it feel to take a life of another?
Murderer... yuh nevah heed the first commandment.

"I'm ready, Easy. Ready for anything." Jigsy's voice was unruffled and full of confidence.

In the back seat, Bluebwai heard Jigsy's every words but they sounded like they were spoken in another time, another place. All yesterday and all this morning, he had felt a cold vibration along his spine. His fingers and toes were tingling. He found himself looking up to the ceiling of the car, wishing for the sky to open and lightening to strike the car. Then it would all be over in seconds. Bluebwai licked his dry lips and glanced at Jigsy behind the steering wheel. He wondered if Jigsy had any idea that he and Storm were related. You just never knew with Jigsy.

ZUKIE REMEMBERED EVERYTHING about the dream which had left him feeling steadily hot and uncomfortable. Since he woke up this morning, panic and desperation were eating away at him. He pulled out the carton of juice from Chico's fridge and poured out his breakfast into a tall glass.

In his dream, it had been the three brothers together, Cliff, Eugene and him. Cliff was explaining how he didn't want to be involved with gangs anymore, but that he was trapped in it and it looked like things were going to get worse from now on.

"Zukie, the ball was rolling down the hill, the minute Fluxy got shot, rolling down the hill gathering people."

Both Zukie and Eugene insisted that they weren't going to sit back while Jigsy was gunning for their brother. It was 'all for one and one for all'. If Jigsy was coming for Cliff, he'd better be prepared to deal with Zukie and Eugene, too. After a brief silence, Zukie asked, "What do you think all this is doing to us — the three of us — as brothers?"

"I think we're getting closer. I think the three of us are getting closer. More like brothers. The way we should have been. It's a shame it had to happen like this," Cliff answered.

"Who do you think's really to blame for all of this?" Eugene asked.

"I don't really know," Zukie replied, sighing.

"Well, I'll tell you. It's Vermont."

Zukie's face creased into a perturbed frown. He wasn't down with blaming the dead man he didn't even know. But Eugene, who knew him, seemed to be sure.

"We should have all been together like one big family. Don't matter if you don't even like each other, you're still flesh and blood and that means you're

225

family, right? If Vermont had made an effort to keep in contact with your side, we could have always been there for each other, helping each other out, even if we didn't like each other that much, right?"

Clifton and Zukie looked at each other, obviously impressed with Eugene's analysis. The boy had hit the nail on the head. They decided that, from now on, they would stick together, help each other out and learn to know and love each other. Their fists met in a punch salute of solidarity, then palms crossing and squeezing. Then they moved closer and hugged, smiling and laughing.

"You haven't smiled like that in years," Clifton told Zukie.

But then things went horribly wrong. Eugene was kidnapped and held hostage by Jigsy, when he discovered that they were related. He threatened to kill Eugene if Clifton didn't agree to a peace talk, to air their differences. It was a hard decision, but Cliff said he had to go. Zukie said he would go with him. They would get out of this together, or they would fall together.

They drove to the meet, which was taking place on wasteland at the top of Moss Lane West, by the crossroads with Withington Road and Upper Chorlton Road, an area known as Brook's Bar.

They should have known it was a trap. Jigsy had been biding his time. When Cliff and Zukie arrived, they were suddenly surrounded on all sides by Piper Mill men who pulled out their guns in broad daylight and gunned the brothers down, laughing as they did so.

Before he awoke from the dream, Zukie heard Jigsy, as he looked down on his peppered body, say, "No one fucks with the Jigs and lives."

Zukie drank the whole litre of juice. He felt fatigued, depleted. His knees were like jelly, barely able to support the rest of him. He suspected something about Eugene Michaels, but for now he didn't know what. All he knew was that the dream was a bad omen.

THE OLD LADY sat proudly in Clifton's sleek new car. He had driven her out of town to Warrington, where the large shopping centres were situated. It had been wonderful to be able to do all the shopping you wanted to do with such a large selection of produce and not have to carry all the bags home. She was proud of her son. This was the way they had been brought up back home, to always take care of the old folk. She had no worries about the future, because she knew that Clifton would be there taking care of her to the end. As they turned into their street, she was so proud as a lot of neighbours were about, and she wanted them all to see how well her son was doing.

Clifton parked a little further down the street, across the road. Parking was always bad on a Saturday. He switched off the engine and jumped out of the car, over to the other side, to hold his mother's door open for her. Today, he was going to treat her like a queen, as she deserved to be treated.

"I'll get the shopping," he said, making his way the boot of the car.

The Old Lady made her way across the road to her

house, walking ten feet tall and thinking she would cook something special for Clifton today. She was overjoyed and proud of Clifton.

"SEE HIM DEH!" Easy cried out triumphantly, pointing excitedly to Storm further down the street. No wonder they hadn't been able to locate him before. But Lewty had told them Storm had changed his car. With the pit bull baring its teeth at him, Lewty was only too willing to co-operate. He eagerly told them as much as he knew. That Storm was lying low and that his mother lived in Hulme, near the Nia Centre building. They'd been driving around for an hour or so, going from one area to another. But Hulme was a big place, undergoing "regeneration", and with so many buildings having come down leaving behind them a wasteland of rubble, it was difficult to follow Lewty's directions. Initially, they concentrated their hunt around the new housing complexes, in front of the Nia Centre Black Arts building off Old Birley Street, then around the new housing estates near Salmon's taxi rank and takeaway close to Denmark Road. They were about to give up when Easy suggested they go back to where they started. If the woman had lived in Hulme for years, he reasoned, she probably lived on one of the older housing estates.

Easy noticed the BMW first, but he wasn't sure it was Storm. Then he saw the fucker, his face half-hidden in a hooded leather parka.

Finally here he is, Jigsy thought, 'Mr Big Shot' Storm, who killed his brother. Well Grangebwai, time's up. Ready for the payback, motherfucker!

STORM TOOK THE plastic carrier bags laden with food out of the boot one by one and placed them on the ground. He heard the quiet, but distinctive sound of a Jaguar further down the road, but he hadn't thought to look up. He should have. The sound of the familiar soft purr of the engine would have ordinarily triggered alarm bells in his head, but he was too concerned with the shopping. By the time he heard the first burst of fire, it was too late.

JIGSY WAS BOTH nervous and excited. Sweat formed on his upper lip, giving his revenge a salty taste. Now, when it was so easy, he began to have his doubts. Then Fluxy's funeral flashed through his mind. He looked across at the faces in the church. Row upon row of black faces, some of which he only saw at weddings or funerals. There were a lot of young faces in the pews, on the balcony above, and at the recesses at the back. Where there were no seats, people were content to stand. He saw the preacher man put on his glasses, then scan the worn, weary faces of the friends and relatives of the dead boy. He heard his mother's weeping, saw her

229

grief. He saw the heads turn as he and his mother walked up the central aisle to pay their last respects, and he saw the coffin, lid down, at the front of the podium.

People were flapping hymn song sheets nervously, agitatedly. He saw Fluxy's girlfriend, heavily pregnant with his child, a sad, remote, lost, vacant look in her eyes. It made his blood run cold.

"There are a lot of old faces in my church today," the preacher said. "Faces I haven't seen in years and probably won't see in church again. I'm not here to preach to nobody. I'm here to teach. Some of you probably don't want to listen. Do you know the story of the shepherd who had a hundred sheep and one got lost? Well, I'm a bit like that shepherd. I'll keep on trying till I've found that lost sheep. Drug gangs and gang warfare. Guns. Extortion. Violence. Intimidation. This is the devil's handiwork. I can see why a lot of you have lost your faith in humanity, but you're making Satan proud. Some people compare this place to Beirut, or New York, the Bronx. Some people compare Moss Side to hell. Hell is all around us. Everywhere. But The Word is mightier than the gun. I have no desire to bury any more boys or girls, cut down in the prime of life. I have a passage from The Bible which I wish to read before we go on to the interment at Southern Cemetery." He paused, catching a deep breath before commencing to read the page from the open Bible on the stand before him.

" 'A good name is better than precious ointment; and the day of death, better than the day of birth. It is better to go to the house of mourning, than the house of feasting; for this is the end of all men, and the living will lay it to heart.

" 'Sorrow is better than laughter, for by sadness of countenance the heart is made glad. The heart of the wise is in the house of mourning; but the heart of fools is in the house of mirth.' "

The memory of the graveside was vivid. Jigsy recalled the graves and tombstones in Southern Cemetery, and the dark clouds overhead, and rain falling like tears from a wounded sky. He remembered feeling the rain beating against his face, but unable to wash away his anguish. His whole body was numb. The faces and bodies all around him were a hazy shade of black. And the preacher's husky voice floating in undulating tones over the wind and rain, and the weeping as Fluxy's coffin was lowered.

" 'For everything there is a season, and a time for every matter under heaven. A time to be born, a time to die; a time to kill, and a time to heal; a time to break down, a time to build up; a time to weep, a time to laugh; a time to mourn, a time to dance, a time to seek, a time to lose; a time to keep, a time to cast away; a time to keep silence, and a time to speak, a time to love, and a time to hate; a time for war, a time for peace, a time to live and a time to die'..."

As Jigsy remembered, he pressed his foot down hard on the accelerator. A mournful cry for his dead brother echoed deep within his soul.

JIGSY ACCELERATED AND Easy-Love gripped the shotgun in both hands, pointing it out the window. Bluebwai in the back seat held the Uzi ready. He leaned forward out of the window and took aim. His mind was ticking away like crazy as time was running out. He in't my brother, he told himself repeatedly. Ever since he was a young kid, he had always wished for a brother, someone to play with, someone to talk to, someone who was closer than a best friend. But Storm was a Grange man. His sworn enemy. He in't my brother, he convinced himself. He's just my father's son. I don't even know him. The Pipers are the only brothers I've known. That was the last thought in his head as he pulled the trigger, and a peaceful Saturday afternoon in Hulme exploded in gunfire.

"OH GOD! MUM! No! Nooo!!" Storm screamed, terror registering in his eyes.

The Old Lady saw the car a fraction of a second before it smashed into her, sending her soaring into the sky. She was thrown clear across the road and landed with a sickening thud on the bonnet of a parked car. She lay there motionless, as the car screeched away around the corner, leaving a trail of mayhem behind it. Stray bullets had shattered the front windows of several houses and the line of parked cars on one side of the road were peppered with bullet holes.

"Mum!" Storm screamed again, this time with pain and despair in his voice, as he ran across the street towards his mother. "No! No, no, no!" he was sobbing even before he reached her.

He feared that she was dead. She lay on the car bonnet completely motionless, her eyes closed. Fortunately, she appeared to be breathing. Storm blinked, relieved to see her chest heaving. She was alive. His heart was beating rapidly, thumping throughout his body. He didn't know what to do next. He told himself not to panic, yet he couldn't believe what had just happened. It took him a moment to figure out the next move. He pulled his mobile out of his inside jacket pocket and dialled 999.

"This is an emergency!" he cried down the line. "Please send an ambulance, quickly. My mum's been knocked down. Please hurry!"

Neighbours soon appeared on the scene. They had heard the gunshots and some of them had even seen Mrs Michaels knocked down. Someone went and got a blanket. Storm didn't know who. He was still in a state of shock, but he had his wits about him enough to scream at anyone who went near his mother. She wasn't to be moved. He knew that. If anybody moved her she could be paralysed for the rest of her life. With fire in his eyes, he swung out at anyone who even considered lifting her off the car bonnet. And in his anxiety for his mother's condition, he forgot all about the gunshots, all about the Jag, all about Jigsy. All he could think about was making sure that his mother pulled through.

"YOU STUPID BUMBOCLAAT eedyat!" Easy-Love screamed. "How could you fuck up like that?!"

Easy was livid. Bluebwai had fucked up big time. They had gone over the plan only briefly, but all Blue needed to remember was that Easy was going to fire the first blast with the shotgun and then Blue was to spray Storm with the Uzi. How simple could it be? Yet, Blue squeezed his trigger too fucking early. They were only half way down the street and had another fifty yards to go. As far as Easy was concerned, Blue deserved some licks for that. He turned to hit him, but Jigsy raised his hand and stopped him.

"Why are you always sticking up for him?" Easy said turning to Jigsy. "Just like Fluxy. Blue fucked up, man. Can't you see that? We fucking hit an old woman!"

Bluebwai didn't say anything. What was there to say? Jigsy didn't feel like talking either, but he did say one thing though:

"Yeah Blue, you fucked up double time, man."

234

T

HE SOUND OF the knocking on the door startled him.

"Zukie!" Chico's mother's voice called from the corridor outside. "Yuh waan breakfast?"

"No thank you, Mrs Anthony!" Zukie called back.

Naked beside him on the mattress, Paradise giggled as she plaited his dreadlocks lovingly. Zukie put his fingers to his lips to tell her to keep quiet, a serious look on his face. Maybe Sister Anthony wouldn't mind him bringing home his girl to stay the night, or maybe she would think he was taking liberties. Either way, he ought to have asked her first.

"I'm going out now, y'hear? I might see you later. Plenty food downstairs."

Half-lying down, his hand propping his head on the pillow, Zukie followed the sound of his landlady's footsteps all the way to the front door. He heard it slam. Then there was silence. Paradise tickled him. He tickled her back. She screamed, trying to push him away. She was more ticklish than he was. He continued relentlessly, until he got his wishes. She agreed to a long, slow, passionate kiss. Soon the kiss became petting, the petting, snogging and the snogging, sexual intimacy. He penetrated deep inside her. Her breath quickened and so did his. She threw her head back, allowing him to caress the base of her neck with his lips, teeth and tongue. He seemed to know all the right spots, his wet tongue exploring her brown body. His movements were rapid, almost frenzied. Perspiration covered both their naked bodies. She was breathless, barely managing sharp gasps and moans. Through her closed eyes, she could feel him sucking and biting her erect nipples and his fingers clawing against her body. Something about him was more mature, more experienced, and he seemed to have developed his technique since the last time. Paradise was suspicious, but said nothing. Zukie had definitely changed. Even after she reached a quivering climax, he waited for her to achieve a second and a third, before he finally gave an involuntary moan of his own.

"Very nice of you to remember me," Paradise said ironically, as they both lay exhausted beneath the sheets on the mattress.

Zukie smiled and accepted that it was a long time since they made love. She had agreed to spend the night with Zukie, despite her father's threat that he would throw her out on the streets, destitute, if she did so. She didn't care. She closed her eyes and leaned back. She still had the hots for Zukie. Her father could throw her out if he wanted to, she would survive. No, Zukie insisted, they would survive, together.

He didn't need to sweet-talk himself back into her life, for he was crazy about her and she obviously felt the same way. Her attitude hadn't changed since the other day, in her garden. She wanted him, wanted to make love to him, so the threats of her father had lost the battle.

Zukie continued to admire his woman.

"So...what am I doing here? What do you want from me?" she asked, teasing.

"Just you," he answered flatly, with a slight tilt of his head, his eyes travelling down to her breasts, jerking as he laughed. The hardness of her nipples, like two sharp points, attracted his eye. Zukie licked his lips.

"Me? What do you want me for? Haven't you got enough problems in your life already?"

Zukie looked away quickly, then directly back at her, keeping her in a cool, steady gaze. He said nothing for a while. Then finally:

"I've got something for you."

He stepped off the mattress, climbed into his boxer shorts, then reached into his overcoat and produced a bottle of expensive perfume. He smiled at her. Paradise smiled back, her eyes glowing. Zukie opened the perfume and sprayed some on his hand. The fragrance filled the room immediately. A romantic and sensual fragrance. Rubbing some on the tip of his nose, Zukie gently caressed her forehead.

"Mmmn," Paradise said, "you smell sweet."

"It's for you," Zukie said, handing her the bottle of perfume. Paradise looked at the bottle and smiled. It was Coco Chanel, an expensive brand. She tied up her hair which was hanging loosely around her neck and shoulders, then sprayed a touch on her neck, dabbing a little on her breasts and shoulders, with a thin finger topped by a long, dark-varnished fingernail.

"Let's take a bath," she said.

Zukie's eyes lit up. Yeah, that was a good idea. He went immediately to run a hot one.

Sitting opposite her in the bath, his back to the taps, Zukie admired his woman, his eyes roving hungrily over every inch of her naked body. Smiling, she turned around and asked him to wash her back. He liked everything about her, including the new hair style. He got the soap and proceeded to lather her back tenderly, paying particular attention to her neck and shoulders.

"We could go away together, you know," he said.

"What do you mean?"

"I mean go away, from here, from Moss Side. Go to London. We could live together, get a job. There's a lot of work in London."

Paradise declared again that she wanted to be with him.

He continued quietly, "I'm looking to the future." His eyes drank in her features.

"Oh yeah? The future, eh?" she asked in a deep Mancunian accent, playfully splashing him with a handful of bath water. "What's that?"

"You, me." Zukie was serious.

Paradise lay back, relaxed in the water, her eyes closed, a satisfying smile on her face.

"THE PROBLEM WITH you, Bow-Bow, is that you leave too much to chance," Edwards was saying. They were down at the police station, in the interview room. Bow-Bow had decided to co-operate. He had waived his right to a lawyer. There wasn't much a legal man could do for a squealer.

Edwards walked to the wall. Pee-Wee had been pushy and assertive, but at least she had sense, which was more than could be said of her man. He nodded to his partner again, who switched on the tape recording.

"Interview resumed at twelve-twenty."

Bow-Bow was a nervous wreck. He was only twenty, but seemed ten years older. His face was pinched and drawn. The years of being a drug dealer and gang leader had taken its toll on him. He was shaking like a leaf, staring ahead at the wall in front of them. He had been here before and he knew the consequences of turning police informer. He looked as if he had given up, like he didn't care about anything anymore.

"I already told you everything I know about the gang-banging," he pleaded.

"Okay." Edwards said slowly, lighting a cigarette and handing it to Bow-Bow. "Guns make you nervous, innit? Since...Jigsy... He really shit you up, didn't he?" Edwards sensed Bow-Bow relaxing a bit. "If you can't take guns anymore, what was this cartridge doing in your flat?"

Bow-Bow looked at the cartridge inside the plastic bag in front of him. He tried to look casual, but his heart was pounding.

"I don't fuck wit it no more," he insisted. "I swear. That was probably there from long time... I don't do those things no more. Drugs dealing is like a noose around my neck, tightening slowly, other drug dealers pulling it. I'm tired of running. I just want to be left alone. I mean, what the hell did I get out of it? I've got nothing of my own. Nothing. The police hounded me day and night... I'm still living in a council house."

Bow-Bow inhaled the smoke from the cigarette, looking directly at Edwards. His large, brown eyes were desperate. He looked like a man condemned, having his last smoke.

"I can't even get a fucking job anywhere, even if I want to go straight," he continued. "They ask me, 'Okay, Mister Watkins, what form of employment have you been doing during the past five years?' What am I supposed to say, 'crack and cocaine representative for a Cheetham Hill Factory'?" Bow-Bow shook his head solemnly. "Believe me, I'm trying to go straight, but it's fucking hard. You can't run away from your past, man. I'm telling you. Anywhere I go. Just last week, I was driving my car and a car draws up next to me. The lights are still on red. A couple of guys look over at me, smiling and waving, the next thing I know is I'm waving at a fucking gun. I bend down just in time and they shoot right through the window before screeching off. A little later on, when I get home, it fucking kicks off there too."

Edwards waited for Bow-Bow to finish his plea for clemency and understanding.

"Save it for the judge," he said finally. "Anyway, you must love it 'cause you still doing it. What I wanna know, is who killed Glenn Ellis?"

"Who?" Bow-Bow asked perplexed.

"Fluxy Ellis," Edwards corrected himself.

"You're not going to pin that one on me, too," Bow-Bow said, laughing, trying to sound casual.

"We've got to pin it on somebody," Edwards shrugged. "You see, this cartridge from your house matches those that blasted Fluxy to hell. Forensics have checked it out. This is now 'Exhibit A'. So what were you doing when he was killed? You see Bow, this in't just a drugs enquiry anymore. This is the big one: murder."

Bow-Bow held his head in his hands and let out a long, slow sigh. He was tired and sick of running. He was a desperate man indeed.

STORM WAS BESIDE himself with grief, but there was nothing else he could achieve by being at the hospital. He felt numbed by disbelief. The Old Lady was on a life-support machine. She was in a coma. The doctors said it was too early to predict her chances of recovery.

It was raining. Pissing down. The wipers swished to the left and right in double time. Driving back from the hospital, Storm could think of nothing but revenge. He was consumed by vengeance. There was no way Jigsy was going to get away with this. This was it...

He couldn't believe how he had let things get this far. If he had dealt with the Pipers swiftly and severely after the attacks on his crew, and the humiliating raids on his operation, the Old Lady wouldn't be lying in a coma. In all the excitement, he had forgotten all about Zukie. But he thought of him now. How was he going to explain this shit to him? Zukie would blame him for everything.

Storm had been trying unsuccessfully to call Lewty's mobile from the hospital. Something about "the vodafone may be switched off." It wasn't like Lewty to keep his line off. He tried again. This time he got through.

"Yo, Lewty. Storm." The phone went dead. Storm frowned. Something was wrong. He punched in Lewty's number on his phone a few more times, before a strong confident voice answered. It wasn't Lewty's.

"Who the fuck is this?" He asked angrily.

"Yaowwww Grangebwai!"

Storm felt his blood run cold. It was Jigsy, alive and kicking and talking on Lewty's mobile. Mocking him while the Old Lady lay critically ill in hospital. How the fuck did Jigsy get Lewty's phone? The image of his mother lying on the hospital bed flashed in his mind. Where the fuck was Lewty?

"So you still deh 'bout?" Jigsy laughed down the line confidently. "How's your mum? It hurts to see your family hurt don't it? Too bad I didn't kill the bitch like you killed Fluxy. I hope you're gonna pay for the damage to my car."

Storm was silent. When he spoke, there was no trace of emotion in his voice.

"What does it feel like to be a dead man, Jigs?"

Jigsy's voice broke with indignation. "I'll kill you first! Save your energy, bwai, yuh gwine need it, to bury all your family. Y'hear me, Grangebwai?"

The connection went dead. Storm snapped his mobile

shut.

"AS LONG AS Jigsy is alive, we're all bumboclaat dead," Bow-Bow sighed, catching his breath. "I thought it was him, Jigsy. I thought Fluxy was him. I shot the wrong brother. I wanted to get him back for what he done to me. If a mad dog was running around loose you would put it down and that's what I wanted to do. It was self-defence, man... But I went and shot the wrong brother. I was careless. I shoulda remembered that Jigsy always wears that fucking scarf around his head."

Edwards nodded in agreement, leaning against the wall of the interview room. He didn't want his man to lose the flow. That's why he had given him a cigarette, to relax him. After repeated interrogations, Bow-Bow was finally confessing. The story was pouring out of him. Pee-Wee had already implicated him anyway, not wanting herself to be involved with a murder case. All Bow-Bow wanted right now was to sleep.

"Look, this is the story," he began, "Fluxy and I had no worries," he continued his voice poised with regret. "He was cool and easy. Easy-Love set the whole thing up..."

Edwards stood up straight. He couldn't believe what he had just heard. "Woah, wait a minute," he interceded quickly, holding up his hand in a halt position. "Wait a minute. Rewind that by me again. Let me get my head around this thing. Easy-Love set it up? Easy-Love the Piper's man, yeah? He set up his own leader? Why...

243

How? Was he there when Fluxy got killed?"

"Me and him..." Bow-Bow pulled on the cigarette. He wished he was smoking something stronger. Everything was coming back to him now, like a video recording in slow-motion playback. "Easy-Love asked me if I wanted to get rid of Jigsy. I said yeah... What choice did I have? He was going around bragging that he was going to do me, that he was going to finish the job off on me, properly, one dark night and soon." Bow-Bow Watkins' voice was little more than a tremble. He remembered it as if it was yesterday. All in the same brief moment he saw the face filled with horror, felt himself squeeze the trigger and the recoil as he let off both barrels. He saw his victim lifted off his feet. But it was Fluxy, not Jigsy. By the time he realised his mistake, it was too late. The memory haunted him. He couldn't have cared less if it was Jigsy. But it was Fluxy lying there.

Bow-Bow put his head in his shaking hands, trying to push the scene from his mind. "I couldn't let that bastard carry on threatening me like that... Easy reached me when I came outta court... asked me if I wanted to get rid of Jigsy..." Bow-Bow continued in a low voice, avoiding the detective's eyes. "He didn't need to ask. I already lost my crew. I was on my own. I had no protection. I couldn't keep looking over my shoulder. Jigsy was bound to catch up with me. What choice did I have? Easy's my cousin, you see, and he was pissed off with the way Jigsy dissed me. So he set up the whole thing and told me where Jigsy was gonna be. Only it wasn't Jigsy."

Edwards thought for a long moment, walked over to the interview table, sat down slowly, then leaned across the table. He looked directly at Bow-Bow. Bow-Bow dropped his gaze.

"Yeah?" Edwards asked. "Surely you in't that dumb?"

Bow-Bow looked up quickly, slightly puzzled.

"What do you mean?" he stuttered.

For a minute Edwards felt sorry for the pint-size villain in front of him. Bow-Bow was a fool. At his age, he should be kicking back with his whole life to look forward to. Instead, he had thrown away his youth and he didn't even know why. As easily as he felt pity, Edwards' emotions became a seething anger. Bow-Bow didn't deserve sympathy, he deserved a slap. How many more black youths was he going to have to lock up? Bow-Bow was just the latest link in an endless chain. Black against black, blood against blood. Why couldn't Bow-Bow see it was madness? Fluxy died for nothing.

Still seething, Edwards clenched and unclenched his fists slowly. He had to remember that he was a professional and that he couldn't allow his emotions to get carried away with him. If Bow-Bow didn't know the runnings by now, then Edwards was going to have to explain it to him.

"Come on Bow-Bow, talk to me. Don't give me all this 'what do you mean' business. I can't help you if you play games. You know what I mean. If Easy knew that Jigsy wasn't going to be there, he set you up. In which case it means he wanted Fluxy out of the way, and he used you to shoot him. You really are that dumb, in't you?"

From his blank expression, Bow-Bow still didn't get it. Edwards tried another tack.

"How did you think Jigsy was going to react when he

245

heard about his brother's death? Who did you think he was going to blame it on?"

All these questions were making Bow-Bow nervous. "He blamed it on the Grange Crew didn't he?" he answered. "That's why the Pipers and Grange have been busting each other up."

"That's it," Edwards said calmly. "Easy must have known that Jigsy would react that way... Maybe that's what Easy wanted? Maybe he wanted a gang war." Edwards' mind was ticking fast. He was clutching at straws, throwing out theories off the top of his head. But it all seemed to have a logic to it which worried him. "Maybe you and he both planned this. Maybe you both wanted the Grange and Pipers to kill each other off, so that you could take control. After all, you and Easy are cousins. And now that you don't have a posse, what could be better than two cousins going into partnership for themselves?" Edwards paused and leaned forward, eyeball to eyeball with his prisoner. "So what do you think Bow, have I got a lively imagination or what?"

At that point Detective Hodge entered the interview room, carrying his green bomber jacket and ready to go.

"I wasn't in partnership with no one!" yelled Bow-Bow.

Edwards was satisfied for the moment.

"Interview concluded at one a.m." He pressed the 'pause' button on the cassette recorder. They needed to make some more enquiries.

"Okay. Delroy, we'll have to check out your story. I'm going to pick up your cousin Easy-Love. And Jigsy too. Then you can tell them what you told me."

Bow-Bow suddenly leaped to his feet, a wild look in

his eyes.

"Nahhh! No way!! Jigsy'll kill me!" he screamed. As if he had just awakened from talking in his sleep and realised that his tongue had been too loose. Talking to the police was bad, but if word got out that he had talked a second time, he wouldn't survive. And if he did, Jigsy would make sure he paid for Fluxy's death for sure. "No way!!! I withdraw my confession!!! I want a lawyer!!! I'll say you made me do it!!! You made me confess!!!"

"We've got it on tape," Edwards reminded him.

"This isn't fair!!" Bow-Bow bawled. "I'm being used!! I want a lawyer!! Get me a lawyer!"

"Good idea," said Edwards. "You're going to need one."

HOW WAS HE going to piece this shit together? His thoughts were on maximum overdrive. Why had Blue pulled the trigger early? Did he diss the programme on purpose? It didn't seem possible. He needed some proof to set himself free from the suspicion. He was thinking so hard his head started to pound. What the hell was happening to him? Was Bluebwai an infiltrator, a spy, a traitor? An informer? A thought crossed his mind that Blue could have even been involved in Fluxy's murder. After all, Blue was there when Fluxy got dussed. And why wasn't Blue covering his brother like he was supposed to...? But the thought was too crazy. It just wasn't possible. If only Fluxy was alive, he would know what to do. Fluxy had been good at sussing things out. But for Jigsy, it wasn't so easy. What was it Fluxy was always saying? "Don't watch the man in front, watch the man behind." What the shit did that mean? You can't walk and look behind, you have to look in front. His head swam. He needed a pull on his coke pipe to clear his mind.

The Jag seemed to swallow up the road. The rain had eased off. There was hardly any traffic around. A police van, siren blasting away, sped past towards the direction of Upper Chorlton Road. They were driving in the opposite direction, down Moss Lane East, towards the heart of Moss Side. The Alexandra Park Housing Estate on their right, Moss Side Fire Station and the Leisure Centre on the left.

They had driven for hours after the hit was messed up. All night long. Easy was still furious. Bluebwai sat in the back, fidgeting, nervous. More questions and thoughts raced in Jigsy's head, swirling around like an overheated pot of hot, peppered soup.

It was dark, but Jigsy could still recognise two of the three youths crossing the road, having a laugh, and sparring with each other and he thought he had seen the light-skinned kid with the brown locks before also. Jigsy slowed the car down and the automatic window slid down. He tooted his horn and shouted, out to the tall dark-skinned youth with the untidy dreadlocks. "Yaowww, Chico!"

Chico came over to the car. "Yes, don!" He saluted Jigsy with a punch greeting.

"Everyt'ing cool?"

Chico nodded. Since the Pipers recruited him to do a

248

bit of dealing on the street, things had been looking up for him. It was small-time stuff, but it was paying him a salary, which was better than living on the dole. Anything was better than living on the dole.

Both Hair Oil and Chico weren't fools though. They didn't intend to spend the rest of their life dealing. They were only going to be doing it for a short time, until they had enough money to set themselves up legit. Enough money to build a recording studio.

"Yuh waan ride?" Jigsy asked.

Chico peered into the car and nodded to Easy and Blue.

"Yeah, we were walking over to Quinney Crescent blues. My bredrin's sound's playing. Pure jungle, you know how dem kids love it. Too much beastbwai 'pon the east side. Appreciate the lift, still."

Chico went back to Hair Oil and Zukie and said that they could get a lift to Quinney Crescent. Hair Oil's freckles spread across his face in a smile and he said that was the way he always liked to arrive, "in fine style." Zukie was less willing to accompany them.

"I didn't know you know dem guys," he said anxiously. "I'm sure they're Piper Mill dealers."

Chico ignored him. "Come on, man," he urged his friends, "they're not going to wait for us all night."

Hair Oil followed him to the car. Zukie stood back, watching them. He would rather walk.

Hair Oil followed Chico back to the Jag and they climbed into the rear seat of the car, sandwiching Bluebwai, with his baseball cap pulled low over his face, in the middle.

Easy turned to Chico. "What happen to your idren?"

249

He indicated Zukie. "Plenty space did deh fe him."

"Don't worry about him, man," Chico replied.

But Jigsy was worried. There was something strangely familiar about the boy.

COLOUR AND FRENCHIE were seated in a little corner of the pub near Sedgeborough Road, talking and drinking, enjoying patties and fried dumplings. In the background, bass-jumping ragga-jungle music played loudly, underground music trying to surface. A shrill purr pierced through the music and their conversation. Both men reached for their mobile phones. Frenchie shook his head. It wasn't his. Colours' Motorola was ringing. He answered.

"Yeah?" Colours had a mouthful of food.

"It's Storm," came the voice at the other end. "I want you to do something, Colours. I want it done, tonight. Jigsy and his crew. All of them, dead. You know his Jag."

Colours smiled at Frenchie, winked and made a gun with his hand. "Yeah," he drawled, "that sounds nice. Now you're sounding like the Storm I know. We shoulda done this weeks ago... No matter, nutting don't happen before the time. Frenchie and I will go with it, y'hear?"

"Another thing," Storm asked. "You hear from Lewty?"

"Nope. Not for a few days."

"Jigsy's got his mobile. So be careful. If you get a call from Lewty, make sure it's him."

EDWARDS FELT UNEASY about the whole situation. He didn't want to let his personal opinions and feelings get in the way of professionalism, but where do you draw the line? Do you stop caring when you become a cop? When one of the officers at the station described Moss Side as "wall to wall shit", it angered him. It mattered to him because Moss Side was his area and his community mattered to him. Talk like that would do nothing to improve police-community relationships.

Edwards sat in the car waiting for Hodge to return. Clearly, Easy-Love wasn't at home. There were no lights on in the fifth floor flat. They had been watching the entrance to the flats, off Bold Street in Old Trafford, for an hour and still no sign of their man. Hodge went up to check anyway, just in case. They weren't having any luck. Jigsy hadn't been in at his place over at the Quays either.

Edwards sighed wearily, leaning his head against the head restraint and looking up at the roof of the car. He looked out of the window again, up towards the fifth floor. Still no lights or movements. He began to reflect on Moss Side again. Gangster business was nothing new in an area with bad housing, poor education and high unemployment. Moss Side had seen its fair share of troubles and riots. But its high percentage of unsolved murders and gun related crimes, stood it apart from many other inner-city areas.

Edwards remembered his father, an ex-Barbadian

police officer, telling him about the gangs back in the fifties and sixties, when the first tide of Commonwealth immigrants came over. In those days, rockers and the teddy boys were the main gangbangers. As well as being small-time criminals, the teds and the rockers spent their time threatening their new black neighbours and deemed certain clubs, cinemas and pool rooms, no go areas to black people. The young immigrants went about in small groups to defend themselves, and eventually formed their own gangs. When the teds and rockers faded out and the black community were well-established in Moss Side and surrounding areas, the fighting became intra-racial. Neighbourhood wars heated up between Africans, Jamaicans and 'Smallies' from Barbados, Trinidad and St. Kitts. Such was the rivalry between the Jamaicans and their fellow Caribbean islanders, that the 'Smallies' often sided with the Africans against the Jamaicans.

All this was before Princess Road became the dual carriage way known as Princess Parkway, to serve those who would rather zoom blinkered through the ghetto. In those days, the Africans owned most of the clubs in Moss Side. Clubs like the Sphinx and the Vegas, out on the frontline when it used to be situated on Princess Road, not far from the old police station, before it was knocked down and the brewery erected in its place. Pubs like the Big Apple and the Old Bristol gradually started to see more black faces. The Dandy Lion pub out on Upper Lloyd Street, previously owned and managed by white people, became a frequent haunt of Yardies and eventually got taken over by them. The Muddy Club also became a popular night spot amongst the new

Jamaicans. It fell into Jamaican ownership, challenging and rivalling the Vegas and the Sphinx. The Africans were reluctant to do business with the Jamaicans and defended their territory to the maximum. Nightly gang battles occurred involving gangs from Cheetham Hill and Africans who drove in from as far as Liverpool. By the mid-seventies things had cooled a bit, but Moss Side's reputation was red hot. Then the African boss of the Sphinx, Musi, got killed over some gambling debts. The Sphinx and Vegas clubs went underground and were eventually taken over by Yardies, and the two clubs' notoriety for prostitutes, rapes, stabbings, drugs dealing, gambling and extortion increased. Soon after, the Vegas and the Sphinx, along with Curly's cafe were pulled down. Rubble was all that remained where they once stood. But their legacy lived on amongst the sons of those first immigrants. These youths were more ruthless and wanted more, much more, than their predecessors. The machetes and cutlasses of old had been swapped for more sophisticated weaponry, and they didn't care about who got caught-up in the cross fire. A cold chill ran down Edwards' spine as he thought about how the city of his youth had changed. No wonder Manchester had acquired the nick-name 'Gunchester'. Then Hodge's knock on the car window, made him jump.

"Let's circle for a bit," the white detective said, "see if we can get some info."

Hodge saw the weary, apprehensive look on his partner's face. He was eager to wrap things up quick, but something told him they were in for a long night.

"You alright?" Hodge asked.

"Yeah, I'm okay. Just a little tired. You drive."

JIGSY SLAMMED HIS foot on the brakes. Everyone in the car lurched forward. Jigsy turned to Blue, who looked very startled, in the back of the car.

Jigsy could feel everyone's questioning eyes on him. He ignored them and concentrated his attention on Bluebwai.

"You know that boy?" He nodded his head back in the direction of the youth with the brown dreadlocks walking over the grass on the street behind them.

Bluebwai feigned ignorance.

"Who, me?"

"Yeah YOU. You know him?"

Bluebwai swallowed, looked directly at Jigsy and shook his head. Jigsy wasn't convinced.

"You know him," he said again. But this time he wasn't asking. He turned to Chico and Hair Oil.

"Who was that youth?"

Chico looked slightly worried. He scratched the bush of hair on his head.

"Er...Zukie...Zuchael Michaels."

Easy wondered what all this was leading up to, but he remained silent.

"Michaels?" Jigsy repeated. He turned to Blue. "You name Michaels too, innit?"

Blue shrugged his shoulders casually.

"Lotsa people called Michaels."

"Yeah," Jigsy said, "but they don't all look like you."

254

THE HOUSE LOOKED strange to him. All this new furniture didn't seem to make sense in the Old Lady's living room. His eyes caught the religious pictures on the wall and everything came rushing back to him.

He could hear the echo of the Old Lady's voice, from somewhere in the past, asking him in her strong Jamaican accent, "Yuh all right?" Her voice, as always, strained with concern. He was reminded of how the sound of her voice always made him jump. But she wasn't here. She was lying critically ill in hospital. He wished he could make time go back. He wished he could undo the past twenty-four hours, but that was impossible. It had happened and it was all his fault. He suddenly hated the house with all its familiarity, its memories, and all the new furniture. He had to fight this strong, compelling urge to smash it all to pieces. He wished he could get in his car and just disappear. He didn't know where. Anywhere. Somewhere. Anywhere far from this place.

Storm decided there was no sense in becoming negative. He had to be positive. He had to rise up again like a storm. Feared and respected by all. This was down to honour now, he had to salvage any respect he had left.

He got to his feet, rising off the settee. His heartbeat felt surprisingly steady as he climbed up the stairs to the room at the top of the Old Lady's house. Once inside his attic bedroom, he leaned against the door for a while, closing his eyes. Then he walked over to his wardrobe, heaving it away from the wall. Breathing heavily, he allowed himself a brief recess before bending down to lift up the carpet underneath. Storm prised the two bits of wood apart. One of the boards loosened. He removed it, revealing a hole. He put his hand down into it. His fingers came into contact with the objects of his search. Metal.

One by one, he took out the small arsenal of arms, examining them. A Browning Hi-Power, a 9mm Glock 17, a Colt .45 and last, but definitely not least, an Uzi. Picking up the Browning, he released the clip of bullets from the handle, checking to make sure it was fully loaded. He reloaded it to make double sure, then tucked the gun into his waist. He put the rest of the weapons into a sports bag.

Storm knew what he had to do. He climbed into his car, carrying the large sports bag. He was prepared to do this on his own if he had to, if Colours and Frenchie didn't find Jigsy before him. A thought came to him as he slipped the key into the ignition. He recalled the hospital number from the mobile phone's memory. There was no improvement in the Old Lady's condition. Storm gritted his teeth and threw the mobile on to the passenger seat. Jigsy was gonna get his! He turned the key and fired up the engine. The wipers came on automatically almost startling him. Another thought came to him. He picked up the mobile and dialled St. Mary's hospital. They put him through to maternity. It was late, but he really needed to talk to his woman. In case anything happened to him, he wanted to give Lalah instructions, how he wanted Tia brought up. He wanted

Lalah to tell her about him when she was older. He wanted Tia to know that whilst he was alive, she was in his thoughts, always.

The ward sister came on the line. She sounded surprised. Lalah and the baby had checked out earlier. Didn't he know? Then he called her number. No answer there either. Where was she? Where was his baby? He snapped the phone shut and gunned the motor. He couldn't waste any more time.

JIGSY WATCHED ZUKIE go on his way. He was deciding what to do. Bluebwai was hiding something. There was no doubt that the two youths were related. Why was Blue denying that he knew the young dread? If his suspicions about Blue weren't aroused by the failed attempt on Storm's life, they were certainly sharpened by all this mystery.

"So Blue, you say you don't know the bwai. Well, I've got an idea."

Everybody in the car was listening intensely. Chico and Hair Oil were wondering why Jigsy wasn't driving them to Quinney. Blue was trying to figure out what he was going to say and do next. Up in the front passenger seat, Easy was confused and didn't know what Jigsy was getting at. Jigsy left them hanging on in suspense as he lit a cigarette.

"I've got a good idea." He puffed out, watching the orange ash glow brightly in the darkened car interior, and turned to Bluebwai in the back. Blue wished he, like the smoke, could curl up and disappear out the window, but he couldn't."I want him."

"What?" Easy-Love snapped.

Jigsy blew out another long puff before answering. "I want him. Here. In the car. I'm gonna have a chat with him to rahtid."

"Cho'!" Easy-Love exclaimed. "What is this, Jigs? We in't got time to go chasing kids around."

"We're not going to do it, Easy." He turned towards Bluebwai. "Blue is."

"How am I going to do that?" Bluebwai asked, helplessly.

Jigsy looked at him icily. Bluebwai saw Jigsy's jaws clench tight. He pulled out his gun and waved it at Blue. "Get him here. Get him now. Get that bwai over here."

Hair Oil and Chico realised that something serious was going down and were becoming decidedly nervous.

"Maybe we should get out an' all," Chico added, pulling out his tam from his back pocket and packing his dreadlocks in it as if he was ready to leave.

"I ain't talking to you!" Jigs snapped.

Bluebwai stepped hesitantly out of the car. Jigsy and Easy watched his every step as he made his way cautiously in Zukie's direction.

"You think he's giving information about our tricks?" Easy asked.

"I don't know." Jigsy's voice was quiet, but tinged with agitation. "I shouldn't have trusted him."

"Well, I wasn't too keen on that white-looking bwai right from the start," Easy said, sniffing as they followed slowly in the Jag, Bluebwai running to catch up with Zukie. "He was an outsider. It was Fluxy who checked for him. We don't know much about his roots do we?"

"I know everything about Blue and you and the other man dem, more than you know about your own selves," Jigsy said.

Easy-Love shifted awkwardly in his seat. Though he knew it wasn't true, the statement nevertheless made him nervous. He wanted to say aloud: "Jigsy, you know jack shit about me." But he didn't. Like his grandma always said, 'keep yuh mout' shut, keep yuh life'!

Jigsy turned to face Hair Oil and Chico in the back.

"So who's this yout' exactly?" he asked.

Chico and Hair Oil shifted uncomfortably, exchanging glances.

"Er... he's just, you know, Zukie. That's all," Chico said, trying to bluff it.

Jigsy made a mental note of that, adding Chico to the list of people he was going to deal with when this was all over. But for now, he kept his mind on little boy Blue.

JIGSY AND EASY were sitting in the car, a few yards away watching the meeting between Zukie and Blue with interest. They were studying the Piper boy's behaviour carefully. A half-hidden 9mm semi-automatic aimed at Bluebwai's spine.

Chico and Hair Oil, in the back of the car, couldn't believe what they were involved with. They wanted to get out of the car, to be far away from the scene. But Jigsy had ordered them to sit tight and they couldn't afford to be seen as anything less than loyal when it came to the Pipers.

Bluebwai contemplated his next move, watching Jigsy from the corner of his eyes. He could run, couldn't he? Warn his brother. But Jigsy's finger was on the trigger and he wasn't known to shoot and miss. He was shaking in his baggy jeans, although he looked steady and confident. He was thinking that he could run up to Zukie, grab him and push him towards the safety of the parked cars, but he decided against it. As Bluebwai approached his half-brother, he became aware of hot sweat on his forehead. He had no idea what he was going to say to the other boy. He didn't know how the other boy would react to him, after all they hadn't exchanged many words at the funeral. They hardly knew each other.

Blue's heartbeat was hammering in his chest, threatening to explode. This is the price of blood, he thought to himself.

Blue called Zukie's name. Zukie spun around, his eyes burning with recognition. He didn't smile. Bluebwai could feel himself perspiring. Zukie regarded him suspiciously.

"Zukie, w'happen? How's things?"

Zukie dropped his eyes to Blue's feet then they looked in each others light-coloured eyes, their inherited legacy, the trademark of their shared ancestry. It was like looking at a mirror image of himself, their features almost identical.

Bluebwai saw the frown steal across Zukie's face.

"You remember me, Zukie?" He looked at Zukie and visualised his old man, Vermont, with him as a child.

Daddy Vermont was always there for him, wasn't he? Drying his tears when he fell, taking turns to wash him in the bath, piggy back rides, stories at bedtime. But he had never been there for Zukie, and Bluebwai felt guilty about that. There was barely a year between them in age, yet life had judged them so differently. He figured he owed his brother something, but he didn't know how he could repay him. Maybe, someday, he would get the chance to have some good times with Zukie, but right now they would both be shot if Zukie didn't co-operate.

"Wanna go for a ride?" he asked, pointing to the Jag behind him.

The boy hesitated, frowning.

"I was just cruising," Blue continued more urgently, "when I saw you. I thought, hey, that's my brother, Zukie. Thought I'd give you a ride, get to know each other more. Anyway, I got something to show you."

Zukie was still unsure. He glanced over at the car.

"It's important. Zukie, trust me," Blue said anxiously, "I'm your brother. I need you to come with me. Please. Trust me. I got no time to explain. Please, trust me." His voice became a pleading whisper. They were taking too much time. Jigsy would be getting suspicious.

"Okay." Zukie finally agreed. Bluebwai sighed with relief, still trying to figure out how he was going to get the two of them out of the situation.

"I seen that car before." Zukie's mind flashed. "That's not your car."

Bluebwai's heart sank.

"You're right, pretty bwai, ah no fe him car!" Jigsy called out, pushing his gun out where Zukie could see it.

261

Confused, Zukie turned backwards to run. But the shout of warning from Bluebwai froze him. Zukie turned slowly back to face Jigsy's toothy grin.

"That's right, rudebwai, you nah go nowhere, right now. So just settle yuhself." Jigsy started to laugh. "Anyway you want it, me can deal the cards."

CLAUSTROPHOBIA. THE CELL was tiny and didn't have windows. Bow-Bow felt closed in. Trapped. What do you do when your back's against the wall and there's no way out, he wondered. He was to remain in police custody with no chance of bail. He knew he didn't stand a chance. Either way, he would have to pay the price for informing. He'd been here before, he just couldn't understand how he had found his way back to this position. Bow-Bow shivered for more reasons than cold.

He would never be able to walk the streets in safety again. He couldn't face prison either. He was a fool to think he could trust people. The police messed him up and so did Easy. He had been used by everyone.

He thought about Pee-Wee saving her own skin at the end of the day. He thought about his daughter. He was going to miss her. But most of all he thought about his own fate. Bow-Bow never really thought he could end up like this again. He was sweating heavily, like someone had turned on a hot-water tap.

He still had his belt. He slipped it off his jeans, his hands shaking, and pulled it taut. Yes, it could definitely take his weight. Somebody laughed outside the cell, breaking his spell for a second, but then the laughter subsided and Bow-Bow continued to ponder his wretched life.

Nobody would miss him. An informer, a junkie. Nobody would care. He was on his own. He tightened his grip on the belt. If you're at the edge of a cliff with an angry crowd chasing you, he thought, you gotta jump.

"YOU INTO RASTA and all that 'thou shalt not steal from thy bredrin'," Jigsy laughed mockingly. Zukie didn't answer. He was still trying to figure out what all this was about. Chico and Hair Oil stared helplessly out of the window at the dark night, wishing they were miles away.

"Personally," Jigsy continued, "I think it's all a load of bollocks, but it's good to have something to believe in, I suppose. Me? I believe in this gun."

He suddenly produced the gun again and aimed it at Zukie's head. Zukie played it cool, staring coldly back into Jigsy's bloodshot eyes. "You not afraid?" Jigsy turned to Easy with a smirk. "Look like we have a bad bwai yah."

Zukie didn't say anything. He remembered the words Bluebwai had said earlier. "Trust me. I'm your brother."

TEEKO MARTIAL WAS getting careless. Confident that things were calm outside, he went for a quick game of pool and a spliff. He paid one of the scouts on a mountain bike to stand in the rain and watch out for anything that looked suspicious, before disappearing inside.

The atmosphere inside the pub was warm and smoky. Hip-hop music was blasting out of the sound system by the busy bar. Young girls, most of them no older than sixteen, hung around waiting to be chatted up. The pub landlord had turned a blind eye to their age, like he had turned a blind eye to the Pipers taking over his pub.

Everything is cool and easy, Teeko thought, as he knocked the red ball into a pocket.

Outside, Storm's BMW pulled slowly into the car park. He surveyed the rows of cars. There was no blue Jaguar. But there was a red, soft top Suzuki jeep.

Storm parked the car. He saw the kid by the entrance watching him and called him over. The boy, not much older than thirteen, frowned and tapped his chest questioningly. Storm nodded with a friendly smile to reassure him. Looking around, the boy approached cautiously. When he was close enough, Storm reached out and snatched the front of his jacket roughly. Fear glowed in the boy's eyes.

"What do you want from me?" His voice trailed out like a long squeak.

"Who's in there?!" Storm roared.

"I can't tell you!"

"They pay you to guard?"

"They'll duss me if I say anything."

"Wrong. I'm going to duss you if you don't start talking." Storm pushed the Browning into the boy's startled face.

"Yuh waan play gangsta? Come play nuh."

The boy started bawling. "Only Teeko," he gulped.

Storm pushed the boy away. The kid got up, dusted himself and, in one movement, picked up his bike, jumped on it and cycled away, as quickly as his legs could pedal. He didn't bother to give a backward glance.

THE JAG PULLED up at Quinney Crescent. Easy-Love kept his gun trained on their hostages in the back seat, Bluebwai and Zukie, trapped together between Hair Oil and Chico. Jigsy climbed out and scanned the group of youths by the door of the blues. He didn't have much time to waste.

"Yaow Danny!" he called across the street, spotting the boy he was looking for. The keen Piper scout jogged over to him.

"Yeah Jigsy, what's up?" the shaven-headed boy asked when he came across. He looked in the car and nodded at Easy through the open front passenger window, and then at Blue in the back seat. He glanced at Chico and Hair Oil. His eyes finally fell on Zukie and a look of puzzlement came across his face.

"You find out anything yet?" Jigsy asked.

" 'Bout what?"

" 'Bout Storm, man. Or any of the Grange man, dem."

Danny looked puzzled and his eyes darted from Jigsy to Zukie and back to Jigsy. He was a good scout who knew most of the players and was usually aware of what was going down. He spent time diligently picking up bits and pieces of information after school by hanging around areas like Alison Street, Graeme Street, Rosebery Street and the frontline on Claremont Road, where most of the dealers, scouts and gangbangers congregated. Teeko had tipped him for future promotion and the boy felt proud and important about being a Piper.

"Well that's his brother you've got back there," he said, pointing at Zukie.

Jigsy nearly choked on his cigarette. Zukie tried to reach for the door handle. But Easy was too quick for him and grabbed Zukie by his locks and pushed the gun to his temple, ordering him to ease back in the seat.

Jigsy climbed back in the Jag, a triumphant look on his face. Easy smiled to himself and hummed his version of a classic ragga rhythm:

"I spy with my little eye, Grange undercover bwai, with dutty dun-dus eye."

266

PURE BAD VIBES filled Frenchie as they sat in their car under the cover of darkness, watching Jigsy converse with Danny briefly, then climb back into the Jaguar. Frenchie felt something was amiss but didn't know what it was. Maybe what bothered him was all the distress his woman had given him. She had been calling him and cussing 'nuff bad word down the line 'bout dis an' dat, and giving him attitude because she hadn't seen him all week and he was neglecting his responsibilities. And another thing, what time was he coming home. Even thinking about it made him angry. He kissed his teeth. It was out of order for her to distress him on his mobile in the middle of a job. As if it wasn't bad enough to call at all, she had rung three times! He was forced finally to switch off the bloody thing as he didn't want his partner thinking that he couldn't manners his woman. Cho, he thought, pure bad vibes!

Things like that didn't bother a hard nut like Colours. Colours wasn't interested in bad vibes. As far as he was concerned, his pump-action would take care of any bad vibes.

If I come home at all, Frenchie thought doubtfully. He kept his eyes on the Jag across the road. It looked like it was rammed full of man. Suppose they were all armed? That would add up to more firepower than the two of them could handle. Colours refused to pick up more soldiers to even things out. He was too eager to get the job done, and confident that they didn't "need no reinforcements to duss a trailerload ah yattyman." Even if they were out-gunned, they still held the element of surprise in their attack.

With a wry smile on his face, Colours loaded the pump-action with the efficiency of someone who had done so many times before. Yeah, this is more like it, he thought. Things had been running slow since he came out of D.C. But now he was back doing what he excelled in — taking on motherfuckers trying to sweat his posse. It was Frenchie's job to drive. Colours was going to do the shooting. He had good eyes and an accurate aim.

It was time to move. The Jag pulled out, with a screech of tyres. Frenchie started the Astra. He and Colours pulled on the hoods of their sweatshirts. He put his foot on the gas and pulled out after the Jag. The shit was about to go down. Payback time.

THE CUE STICK tore into the side of Teeko's skull as Teeko's grip on the side of the pool table weakened. He fell, stunned. Storm pulled out his gun and waved it about. Most of the regulars ran from the pub screaming, a handful were frozen with fear, unable to make a move.

Teeko reacted so quickly that he took Storm by surprise. The Piper Mill lifted himself up with all his strength, driving his clenched fist hard between Storm's legs at the same time. Storm doubled in pain. Still groggy, Teeko fled from the pub. Storm caught up with Teeko easily enough in the car park, trying to fit his key into the lock on the driver's side of the red jeep. Storm

snatched him by the neck and hurled him to the ground.
They rolled and struggled for control, but Storm
overpowered him.

"Get up," Storm ordered.

Teeko raised himself unsteadily, breathless and
bleeding from the head. Storm's gun was trained level at
his forehead. Teeko felt himself tremble, but maintained
his cool as best as he could under the circumstances.

"I've got no gun, man, what you going to do? Shoot a
man without a gun?"

Storm wasn't angry, he was raging.

"You didn't give my mum a chance when you
knocked her down. Why should I give a fuck if you
haven't got a gun?"

"What are you talking about? I wasn't there. I never
knocked down no woman. That ain't my style... But if
you want a fair fight, here I am. Take me, a fair fight
right?"

"What the fuck are you talking about?" Storm
wondered whether Teeko was laughing at him. "Why the
fuck should I want a fair fight?"

"I just thought you might like a fair fight," Teeko
said, seriously.

"Fuck fair fights!"

"Just like I figured," Teeko said quietly, "you're a
coward. Maybe you'd like to shoot me and run, like you
did Fluxy."

Teeko's frightened eyes were fixed on Storm's finger
on the trigger. He saw the blood seeping down from the
wound on the side of the boy's head. Teeko was
panicking.

"What yuh waiting for?" he screamed slightly

hysterically. "Can't you do it? Do it Grangebwai. Do it! Waste me!!"

Something deep within Storm pulled. His conscience tortured him. He couldn't do it. His finger hovered over the trigger of his gun. He couldn't do it.

Teeko turned his back slowly, taking advantage of the hesitation to walk away. He knew that if Storm had taken this long, he wouldn't do it.

"What the fuck?" Storm addressed the question more to himself than Teeko. But he didn't do anything. From the pub behind him, he heard the screams and shouts of the remaining regulars as they fled. They would have to find somewhere else to enjoy a quiet pint. Teeko kept walking.

"Teeko!" Storm called out finally.

In the brief moment that the youth turned around, Storm squeezed the trigger of his gun and pumped three shots into Teeko. Teeko staggered about, clutching his chest, before falling to the ground.

Storm didn't hang around. He needed to get out of there fast.

Lying on the ground, Teeko heard his attacker's hurried footsteps and heard the roar of the engine as Storm sped away. Teeko listened as the car faded in the distance. When all was safe, he got up casually and dusted himself down. Next he examined the three fresh holes in his bulletproof vest.

THE POWERFUL CAR slid easily through the streets.

270

Rain snapped on the windscreen, swishing at the tyres. Riding the strong reggae pepperseed rhythm with nippy lyrics, Bounty Hunter was pumping out of the stereo system so loud that it was impossible to hear anything else. Despite the deafening sound, Zukie's mind, was concentrated on the fear that Easy's gun, still aimed at the back seat passengers, commanded. Zukie's heart beat so fast it threatened to explode. This really was happening, and it was happening to him. All his life he had tried to stay away from this kind of business and here he was, caught in the middle of his two brothers and their gang t'ing. Why did Eugene have to involve him in this bad bwai business? Though frightened, Zukie's mind was focused. He was not his brothers' keeper. They could live their lives and he would live his.

Jigsy re-adjusted the volume on the car stereo to an acceptable level. With one hand on the steering wheel, he took out Lewty's phone. It was similar to his, sophisticated and expensive. He flicked it open and found Storm's mobile number in its memory. He called the number. As he waited for a connection, he glanced in the rearview mirror and caught Blue glaring at him in a defiant pose. Jigsy chuckled to himself. Come soon, starbwai, come soon. Then Storm answered at the other end.

"Yaow Grangebwai...! Pussyhole!"

That's all Jigsy managed to say before a stream of profanities greeted him from down the line. He turned his ear from the phone for a moment, holding it away and smiled at Easy.

"Sound's like Storm's become a hurricane."

Easy laughed a hollow laugh. Jigsy listened to the abuse. Then it was his turn to speak.

"No you listen to me motherfucker! We've played enough games with you and your boys. I said what I was going to do and I meant it. I got your brothers. We know all about you. I got them here in the car with us... Yeah, the dreadlocks, Zukie and the other one, Bluebwai, Eugene or wha' de raas yuh waan call him. So in case you're planning a counteraction for what happened to your mother, back the fuck up!"

Jigsy didn't bother waiting to Storm's response. He was laughing so hard he nearly dropped the phone. Storm was trying to tell him they were going to be hit, but Jigsy was too busy laughing. He snapped the phone shut then turned to Bluebwai and Zukie.

"You motherfuckers are my insurance policy. Seen?"

Zukie was seething with anger. Easy saw the look on his face and waved the gun threateningly in front of him, just in case.

"My mother? What the fuck did you do to my mother?!" Zukie said his voice taking on a breathless urgency. He wanted to pounce on Jigsy, strangle every breath of air out of him, but he was in no doubt that Easy would use the gun on him if he tried anything.

Jigsy stared at the road ahead. They were on Alexandra Road South, heading towards Mauldeth Road West, the dual carriageway near Hough End playing fields.

"Your mother decided to take a walk in front of my jag," he said coldly, readjusting the bandanna on his head with one hand.

Zukie felt helpless. His world was being turned

upside down and there wasn't a damn thing he could do about it. Bluebwai turned to his brother. He saw the despair in Zukie's face and wished he could turn back the hands of time. He should have blasted Jigsy and Easy when he had the time. Now it was too late. All he could do was squeeze his brother's hand gently to support him.

"SORRY. THE CELL phone you are calling may be switched off. Please try again later."

Storm listened to the message, panic and frustration rising with each pre-recorded word. He didn't know whether Jigsy had taken the Jag off the streets, and he couldn't get through to Colours or Frenchie. He was desperate. He had to call off the hit. He had to let Colours know that his brother was with Jigsy and it was too risky. He had a chance to stop things turning really bad if he could only get through to someone. He tried again to reach Jigsy on Lewty's mobile, but no joy there either. His hands were sweating. A cold sweat. What was he going to do? His mind throbbed with possibilities. Maybe Frenchie and Colours hadn't tracked Jigsy down yet. Maybe Jigsy was lying. Maybe Zukie wasn't in the car. Maybe! Maybe! MAYBE!! There were so many thoughts running through his mind he couldn't think.

Storm felt helpless. His hands shook with fear. How the fuck did Zukie get mixed up in all this? Eugene was in the car also, but Storm was more concerned about

Zukie. Eugene might be his brother, but not in the way Zukie was.

He couldn't think of anything better to do than call in his scouts. He dialled Kirk's number. The boy was asleep at his parents' house, but his sister woke him up. Storm spoke to him briefly. Told him to get some of his friends together. Tonight he needed them for a different purpose. Tonight he needed them to help him search for Jigsy's car. It was an emergency. On their mountain bikes, they were fast. Storm himself would go over to Cowesby Street to see if he could pick up the trail from there.

THERE WASN'T MUCH traffic on the road at this time of night, but Chico noticed the headlights behind them. He first saw them in the side mirror. The car lights had been sitting comfortably behind them for the last few minutes. Terrified of the situation he was now in, he didn't know whether to mention it to Jigsy or not. He was certain that there was a car tailing them. His throat was so dry he swallowed thin air. Finally he said it, stuttering nervously.

"I th..think someone's f..following us."

"Where?!" Easy shouted, turning and peering out the rear windscreen anxiously with a squint. This was not what he wanted at all. "Jigsy, you speeding?" he asked.

Jigsy glanced at the rear-view mirror.

"It in't no police," he said, taking out the gun from his waistband. "They woulda flashed long time and pulled

274

us over."

He looked in the mirror again as he pushed the gas pedal down. "Let's see what kinda firepower those motherfuckers got," he said, with a chuckle.

Jigsy took a sharp right with a screech of burning rubber, and swung the car onto the open dual carriageway. He gunned the Jag up to sixty, then seventy, easily. The car behind stuck to them like white on rice.

"This is a hit, Jigsy!" Easy screamed, picking up the Uzi on the floor in front of him, and hitting the button for the automatic windows to slide down. Zukie's heart thudded. Everything seemed to be happening in slow motion. They say when you think you're about to die, your whole life flashes past in an instant. Things you did, things you said, things you wished you had said, people you hurt, people you love. Zukie saw all these things. On either side of him, Chico and Hair Oil were shaking with fear. Bluebwai sat paralysed.

Easy leaned out the window, as far as he could and took aim. At the wheel, Jigsy still had his foot all the way down on the gas pedal and, doing ninety, it was difficult keeping the Jag straight. Easy didn't have time to pull the trigger before the headlights from the pursuing car illuminated him in a floodlight of full beam. In the back seat of the Jag, the hostages didn't have to be told to keep their heads down. The headlights had made them a sitting target.

"Take out those fucking lights!" Jigsy barked.

Easy squinted but all he could see was two blurs of blinding, white light. He aimed at what he thought was the centre and let off a short burst of gunfire. But the

275

headlights were still right behind. He squeezed the trigger again, but this time all he heard was a click. What the ff...! He squeezed again, and again and again, but nothing. Without warning the sound of pump-action shotgun fire exploded into the air, at the same time as the Jag's rear windscreen shattered in a million pieces. The pump-action blasted again and this time it tore into the back of Jigsy's head, leaving a hole the size of a fist, and covering the windscreen with bits of his brain. Jigsy slumped down over the steering wheel, triggering the horn to sound in a loud, haunting monotone. Keeping their heads well low, the hostages in the rear seat were trapped in the crossfire. They didn't know what was happening but they knew that something was seriously wrong, as the Jag swerved to the left then to the right, zig-zagging erratically across the carriageway. It careered across to the central reservation and struck the barrier at an angle, which flipped the Jag over and sent it spinning on its roof. The Jag finally came to a rest in the middle of the dual carriageway. The car behind was forced to brake hard. The two assassins got out of the car quickly and briefly surveyed. Frenchie was nervous like fuck, and looked up and down the dual carriageway to see if any cars were coming. Luckily there were only a few cars on the other side of the reservation and none of them stopped.

"Let's go. Come on!" he urged his partner. "Now, Colours. No one woulda survived."

Colours shook his head. "We've got to wrap it up. No loose ends."

"Fuck that!" Frenchie pleaded. "None of them are getting out of that alive. Let's just get the fuck out before beastbwai come!"

The glare of a car's headlamp coming down the road behind them made the matter more urgent. Frenchie tugged Colours by the sleeve and they quickly climbed back in their car, speeding away with a screech of tyres.

THEY WERE BACK at Easy's flat on Bold Street, hoping they could find their man. Edwards was ready to call it a night when the alert came through from the station of gunshots in the vicinity. Edwards looked at his partner. Hodge nodded, they weren't far from the dual carriageway. If they got onto Alexandra Road South they'd be there in minutes.

No matter how much firearms training you get nothing can prepare a policeman for the real thing. Edwards' adrenaline pumped fast, his heart beat hard, and the palms of his hands began to sweat. They were going into the unknown and didn't know what would be waiting for them at the scene of the incident. That always made him nervous. They couldn't afford any mistakes. In training you don't get shot by real bullets, you can roll over and 'die', get up and walk away. Even wearing the standard bullet-proof vests wasn't enough to ease his nerves. There was always a chance of getting a bullet in the neck or the head. Despite the fear, it was his job and he had to do it. He tried to push the fears out of his mind and concentrate on the road ahead.

EASY WASN'T PREPARED to accept that it was all over for him. The way he saw it, he had been lucky. If he wasn't leaning out of the car when it flipped, he would have been trapped inside with the others. Instead, he was thrown clear into a ditch at the side of the road, where he lay absolutely still, grazed, dazed, but still alive. He waited until he heard the two assassins speed off, before he got up stiffly. His legs were weak but he knew he had to get away. The police would be on the scene soon and he didn't want to be around when they arrived. It didn't take him long to find the Uzi, lying a short distance away. He picked it up and limped his way to the road where the Jag still lay on its roof. The first car that came barely slowed down as it approached the wreck of the car in its path. The driver swerved around the obstacle and continued down the road. Easy hid the Uzi behind his back and flagged the second car down as it approached. The car screeched to a halt. Easy limped over to the driver's side and pointed to the wreck of the Jag a short distance down the road and shouted, "There's been an accident, I'm hurt... please help me. The two men in the car looked at each other, puzzled. Easy waited for the man to wind down his window before producing the Uzi.

"Right, don't make a fucking move if you love life... Open up the back door and don't even think of trying any fast moves."

Easy noticed the trickle of water on the driver's temple, saw the fear in his and his passenger's eyes. This is going to be simple, he thought. He jumped in the back as soon as the driver lifted the lock button.

"Right, here's the rules," Easy continued, once he was

comfortably in the back seat, "I'm the fucking boss, I give the orders 'cause I got this."

He jammed the Uzi muzzle in the back of the driver's head. The driver, a young black man in his late twenties, yelled with pain.

"You wanna see what it feels like if you try and fuck me about... So drive and just keep driving... I'll tell you the way," he said. He smiled to himself briefly. Even with an Uzi which had jammed, he could command respect.

Somewhere in the distance, the wail of police and ambulance sirens pierced through the quiet night air coming in their direction. "Move it!" Easy ordered. The driver did as he was told. He swerved past the wreck on the road and continued down the dual carriageway. His passenger, a well-built white man in a green bomber jacket, was a few years older. He did as he was told also and kept his eyes on the road. Easy didn't want either of them looking at him too tough and being able to identify him later. He barked the directions unceremoniously. In the front seats, detectives Edwards and Hodge looked at each other briefly. That's him, they were both thinking. That's him! This was the man they'd been looking for. But what could they do with an Uzi pointing straight at them? Edwards knew now that he was going to get his man, but he also knew that Easy would shoot his way out if he had to.

BLUEBWAI'S FIRST THOUGHT was that he was

alive. Trapped upside down in the wreck with somebody on top of him, he couldn't move. But thank God he was alive. He shivered. He was breathing with difficulty, in deep heaves, and he could taste the blood in his mouth, but he was comforted by being able to feel his arms and legs. His second thought was for his brother. Was he dead or alive?

"Zukie!" he groaned in a hoarse whisper. "Zukie... can you hear me!"

"Www...what happened?" came a reply from the person on top of him, but it wasn't Zukie. Blue recognised Chico's voice. Then he heard the echo of emergency sirens approaching. It sounded like several vehicles.

THE STREETS WERE crawling with cops. Tears filled Storm's eyes as he drove hastily towards the hospital. Colours had confirmed the hit and Kirk, one of his young scouts, had called him on the mobile to say that news of the shooting was already buzzing on the frontline, and that someone had seen ambulances race from the scene in the direction of M.R.I. But was Zukie okay? Storm needed to know. He was desperate. Kirk hadn't heard anything about Zukie, and nobody could confirm whether the Jag's passengers were dead or alive.

Storm feared the worse. As if he knew his brother was dead, black and white memories of the past were flashing through his mind. Images of Zukie playing football, Zukie on his first bike, and smiling school photo images of Zukie in his uniform, without dreadlocks. Zukie had always been a handsome kid. Storm began sobbing. What had happened to his brother? Had he ordered his own brother's killing? Why had this happened to him? What had he done to deserve this? His emotions ranged from fear and grief, despair and heavy guilt. For the first time in years, he begged God to let Zukie live, and made a silent pact to do anything, anything, if only God would let Zukie live. As if he was waking up from a long sleep, he began to realise the full meaning of the last few days' events. He had destroyed everything that he loved, and one by one, those he loved had left him. Lalah and Jasmine had disappeared with his children because of the life he lived, and the Old Lady was lying in hospital because of him. And now his brothers had been shot, also because of him. That wasn't all. He had plenty more disasters to choose from. Other people had suffered as well, not just those who were injured or killed, but their families too and their friends also. He thought about Zukie and Bluebwai. Even if they were alive, they would hate him for ordering the hit that resulted in their injuries. They would probably never want to see him again. One way or another, he had lost them.

EASY ORDERED THE driver to pull up across the road to his block of flats in Bold Street, after having been forced to take the back streets because the cops were everywhere. He had to get home, get off the streets

281

and to pick up a gun that fired.

"Okay you motherfuckers," he said, "you're lucky I'm in a good mood. Just keep driving after I get out. I know your registration number and if I get to hear that you've been speaking to the cops about me, I'll find you. And next time, I won't be so polite."

Without another word, he climbed out of the car still carrying his Uzi. He hadn't taken more than a few steps across the road, before a call stopped him dead in his tracks.

"STOP! ARMED POLICE!" The shrill cry echoed in his ears. Easy turned around slowly to face the driver and his passenger, both with handguns drawn and taking cover behind the car. A puzzled look formed on Easy's face. He looked at them both and something told him that this was for real. He looked down at his Uzi. Maybe he could still luff it.

"Don't even think about it!" Edwards shouted. "Drop the gun... SLOWLY!"

Easy smiled and let the Uzi slip through his fingers. It dropped to the ground with a crash.

"It don't work anyway," he laughed. "It don't fucking work!"

Unsmiling, Edwards kept his gun trained on the youth. Hodge did the honours and walked around the car to cuff Easy, then he read him his rights, before pushing him into the back seat of the car. The detectives climbed in after him. Edwards pulled out his walkie-talkie and radioed the station with the good news. The desk sergeant replied that they had called off the hunt for Marvin Ellis. He had been shot dead. They had found him in the wreck of the car that turned over on the dual carriageway. Four other youths in the car survived and had been taken to the M.R.I.

With a cold look in his eye, Edwards turned to Easy in the back seat. "I suppose you're proud of all the fuckries you've caused by having Fluxy shot? I bet you just love it, don't you?"

"Yeah that's right beastbwai," Easy laughed, "but what I loved the most was taking a couple of cops hostage with a gun that can't fire. Aaaaagh, ha ha ha!"

T HE OLD LADY lay on her back in the hospital, her eyes cold, drifting back to the golden country. Vermont was on the other side of the river with their children Grace, Phillip and Neville, back home in Jamaica, in their old village, Bluefields, in Westmoreland. She didn't know how she had got there but she was happy. The air was fresh and clean, extremely refreshing. The sun was shining, there were birds flying above in the sky, and the women-folk with their scarfed-heads down gossiped, laughed and chatted loudly as they washed their laundry in the river. She had been here many times before in her dreams and heard the women's stories over and over again. She even recognised the voices of people she hadn't seen in years: Cynthia, an old school friend, Margaret, Blossom, Miss Tom, Miss Irene and a few others. But none of them recognised her.

She called out to Vermont on the other side. He didn't seem to hear her, neither did the kids. She called again, this time much louder and more anxiously, but still

Vermont did not respond. He turned his back on the river and made his way up the gully away from her. She called out repeatedly, "Monty! Monty! Monty!!" But it was no use, he just kept walking, taking the kids with him.

She was still calling out for Monty when she was gently woken by Clifton.

"Mum, it's alright, it's alright. I'm here with you."

She opened her eyes and saw her son's reassuring smile looking down at her. He had brought her flowers and fruit.

"Cliff, yuh mus' try and talk to Zukie. Tell him to come home. I want us to be a family again. An' yuh mus' contact your sister and brothers in America and Canada. And the other pickney too, your daddy's other son. And no matter what, you take care of all of them. Blood thicker than water, yuh know."

Storm winced with pain at his mother's words. He wouldn't be able to hide things from her for much longer.

Single Black Female

By Yvette Richards

When thirtysomething **CAROL'S** marriage ends dramatically, she gives up on men and is convinced she'll never find happiness again.

American advertising executive **DEE** moves to London looking for new horizons and maybe 'Mr Right.'

DONNA leaves an empty relationship in Bristol and heads to the Capital in the hope of making it big as a model.

They all end up sharing a house and soon discover that black women wherever they're from, have the same problem...**MEN**!

Together they experience the ups and downs of single life in the 90's. They finally discover that something special can happen with a man when you least expect it.

"Excellent...no woman's bookcase should be without this hugely entertaining and uplifting novel."
THE VOICE

"A compulsive read... written with humour, Single Black Female hits us men with some real home truths."
PATRICK AUGUSTUS

"Yvette Richards 'tells it how it is' and entertains with a story that echoes the experiences of women from all walks of life."
PRIDE MAGAZINE

The
Ragga
&
The Royal

"Monarchy will never seem the same again. A hilarious mick take of the British class system"
THE VOICE

"Surely one of the funniest and most outrageous comedy novels for years. Even the Queen would have to smile."
PAPERBACKS REVIEWED

WHEN The Princess decides to include inner city problems as part of her charitable work, little does she know where it'll end!

As 'community representative' at a large urban development project, Leroy Massop is about to start working very closely with The Princess on her charitable mission.

They are worlds apart but The Princess is taken by his streetwise charm. Soon a cool working relationship starts to develop into something a lot hotter!

It's an illicit liaison that could destroy the monarchy and her husband, The Prince, is determined that it MUST be stopped. In the meantime Leroy is desperately trying to keep not only his long-term woman sweet, but his 'runnings' as well!

THE HOT NEW BOOK BY **Monica Grant**

Black Classics

THE BLACKER THE BERRY
by Wallace Thurman

Emma Lou was born black. Too black for her own comfort and that of her social-climbing wannabe family. Resented by those closest to her, she runs from her small hometown to Los Angeles and then to Harlem of the 1920's, seeking her identity and an escape from the pressures of the black community.
She drifts from one loveless relationship to another in the search for herself and a place in society where prejudice towards her comes not only from whites, but from her own race!

First published in 1929, The Blacker The Berry, caused a storm when it was released. It dared to say what everyone in black America knew, but didn't want to admit. For many years it has remained a lost classic in the vault of black literature but its "raw and penetrating insight" has as much relevance for the black community today, as it did decades ago.

IOLA by Frances E.W. Harper

The beautiful Iola Leroy is duped into slavery after the death of her father but the chaos caused by the bloody American Civil War gives her the chance to snatch her freedom and start the long search for the mother whom she was separated from on the slave trader's block.
With the war unfolding around her, Iola endures her hardships with a growing pride in her race. Twice she rejects the advances of a white doctor, who offers to relieve her from the "burden of blackness" by marrying her, and chooses instead to devote herself to the upliftment of her people. It's here that she eventually finds the true love she has been seeking all her life.

Iola was the most widely read black novel of the 19th century and was hugely influential in high-lighting the plight of black American slaves. It was also the first novel which featured a black woman as heroine and was an inspiration for many later black writers.

THE
VICTOR HEADLEY
COLLECTION

3 Tuff Novels From The Number One Black Author In The UK:

YARDIE

At Heathrow Airport's busy Immigration desk, a newly arrived
Jamaican strolls through with a kilo of top-grade cocaine strapped to
his body. And keeps on walking...
By the time the syndicate get to hear about the missing consignment,
D. is in business — for himself — as the Front Line's newest don. But
D.'s treachery will never be forgotten — or forgiven. The message filters
down from the Yardie crime lords to their soldiers on the streets:
Find D. Find the merchandise. And make him pay for his sins...

EXCE$$ – THE SEQUEL TO YARDIE

Things got really hot after D.'s arrest. The police virtually closed
down Hackney for business. The posses have had to take stock
and regroup. But the shaky truce that followed their turf war, is
getting shakier as Sticks, a 9mm 'matic in his waist, dips deeper
and deeper into his own supply of crack...

YUSH! –THE FINAL SCORE

The final curtain comes down on the superb Yardie trilogy. An all guns
blasting end, worthy of Britain's most popular black writer. If you enjoyed
reading it remember to big up the book to your bredrin.